Your Guiding Genius

Building a World Class Team

by

Jay LaBonte

Pinecone Publishing
Boca Raton, Florida

Visit my web site at www.jaylabonte.com

First Edition

ISBN: 978-0-615-26425-7

I dedicate this book to my father, Jack Leonard LaBonte (1922–2006). When I started my first business, he presented me with a plaque with the following inscription:

> Make no small plans. They have no magic to stir man's blood and probably themselves will not be realized.
>
> Make big plans; aim high in hope and work, remembering that a noble, logical plan once recorded will never die, but long after we are gone will be a living thing, asserting itself with ever growing insistency.
>
> Remember that our sons and daughters are going to do things that will stagger us.
>
> Let your watchword be order and your beacon, beauty.
>
> Think BIG.
>
> —*Daniel Burnham*

He lived by this motto, and all he did evidently reflected it. My father was not just a dreamer, but also a doer, and it is with great pride that I have written this book in memory of my father so that the lessons he taught me can be passed on for generations to come.

Table of Contents

Acknowledgements

The task of writing a book is not an easy one and can take years to complete. With each new book, an author refines his style, and I am no different. I must thank my friend and author, Robert Ringer, for his valuable advice, insights, guidance, and honesty that helped me take this book from a collection of notes and a rough manuscript to its final form.

I also extend my sincere thanks to my editor Susan Andres for her keen eye and skillful editing of my manuscript.

Finally, I could not have done any of this without the support and encouragement of my loving wife Kathleen who, for better or worse, stuck by me as I worked many long hours to complete this book.

Introduction

In 1905, Albert Einstein developed his theory of special relativity, proving that atoms exist and determining that light behaves as both a particle and a wave. And to top it all off, at the age of twenty-six, he developed his famous equation $E = mc^2$, which describes the relationship between matter and energy. Einstein was a genius, and I do not think anyone would argue that. But Einstein was not the only famous genius. Isaac Newton is commonly known as the father of physics and developed the form of mathematics known as calculus. Wolfgang Amadeus Mozart was also a genius who started composing music when he was only five years old. Before his death in 1760 at age thirty-five, he had written hundreds of musical compositions.

But these are examples of outstanding geniuses. Other forms of genius are not as well known as Einstein or Mozart. They are the everyday geniuses that live and work just like everyone else. They may not be mathematical or musical geniuses, and they may not be able to invent breakthrough technologies, but they are geniuses just the same. Most people think spotting a genius is a rather simple task, believing geniuses are rather eccentric or have quirky behavior. But the truth is there are geniuses all around you; in fact, you may be one of them yourself and not even know it.

Many people think that genius is measured by the level of someone's intelligence based on standardized intelligence quotient or I.Q. tests. But I.Q. tests only measure a portion of a person's total intelligence, and in many cases, there is no accurate way to test a person's real genius. Genius is a big picture concept that involves more than measuring a person's intelligence and his ability to learn and process information.

As explained earlier, Mozart was a genius but that does not mean he could have created calculus as Isaac Newton did, just as Isaac Newton could not have comprehended Einstein's theory of special relativity. Simply being a genius does not mean you have all the knowledge in the universe; it means you have a different way of looking at a given problem and arriving at a solution.

Defining how genius works is a subject that goes well beyond the confines of this book. Therefore, for the sake of this book, a genius is not simply a person with an exceptionally high I.Q., but is a person that breaks new ground, whether it is a new discovery, an invention, or a management technique. Yes, I said management. Usually a genius' work changes the way people view the world or the field in which the work took place, or in your case, how your team views the work to be done.

So what makes you a genius? Is it a different, more agile brain? Is it an exceptional intelligence? Is it an aptitude for noticing information that other people might consider irrelevant? Is it your ability to motivate people to perform at their peak? The answer is all of the above or any of the above.

There is a big difference between being exceptionally smart and being a genius. A smart person may know many facts, may be able to perform learned tasks with great skill, or be able to understand how to program a computer or construct a house. But a genius uses his imagination and creativity to discover or create something new or even to figure out how to motivate someone that otherwise cannot be motivated. Geniuses break new ground rather than simply remember or recite existing information.

Have you ever met a salesperson that could sell a glass of water to a drowning man? If you have, that is a sales genius, or the CEO that can bring a company from the brink of bankruptcy to record profits—that is a business genius. Or the nurse that can manage a waiting room of sick, irritated, demanding patients and keep the doctor on schedule—that nurse is a genius as well. Geniuses exist in all occupations and all business venues.

Management geniuses do not operate in isolation, handing down orders and process improvements. Management geniuses work hand-in-hand with their team of geniuses in a collaborative effort, allowing their team members to grow. You can find genius in everyone on your team—the genius salesperson, the genius programmer, or the genius bookkeeper. The key is finding the genius in each of your team members and then nurturing it. In this book, you will find proven techniques, strategies, and pointers to help you find and nurture the genius in each one of your team members, as well as your own genius as a team manager.

Your Role as Team Leader

Every team needs a good team leader, a leader that can keep the team focused and keep communications open and flowing in both directions.

Many people have asked me to define the perfect team leader or describe the perfect team leader's personality and traits, so they can try to identify good leaders before they make them leaders.

The problem is that there is no pre-defined guideline as to what makes a good leader, or even a great leader, other than they have the team's interests in mind. It is, however, much easier to describe the various negative types of team leaders and the traits that each type demonstrates so that you may better understand what does not work in managing a team.

Presented here is a list of the twelve negative types of leaders.

#1—The Fearful Leader

Upper management persuaded this leader into taking the position simply because management decided that there should be a team leader, and they wanted someone they could assign duties to that would not answer back. This leader is too timid to ask to be re-assigned or to let management know that he cannot perform the task of being a team leader. He spends most of his time worrying about the job and being fired. This type of leader is generally a good person and tries to do a good job but lacks the backbone to deal with poor decision by upper management.

#2—The Informant Leader

This type of leader does not think for himself and takes every word handed to him from upper management as gospel. When someone on his team disagrees with a management decision, he is quick to apologize for this team member's blasphemous statements. Even more worrisome is the fact that he reports every comment he hears back to management. This type of leader would feel perfectly at home as a member of the KGB's secret police. This type of leader is a perfect candidate for negative office politics and is often used for spreading propaganda.

#3—The Egotistical Leader

This leader thinks that he has arrived. He assumes all eyes are on him, and he will save the day. He believes that all he touches turns to gold, and everyone should listen to his every word.

If you have not figured it out yet, this leader is full of himself. If you have ever had a leader such as this, you may have actually heard him speak about himself in the third person. When speaking of other senior managers of the company, he will refer to them as his colleagues or "fellow members of the management team," thereby letting you know he is above you in the company hierarchy.

#4—The Cave Man Leader

This type of leader is mostly found in the technology field, and he lives, eats, and breathes technology. Generally, the technology is computer-related. At the end of the day, the cave man leader goes home to his technology cave where he spends most, if not all, of his off-duty time working on his own technology. It is a good bet that this type of leader has attended a Star Trek convention on various occasions or has some other unhealthy obsession in the realm of science fiction that goes well beyond simple relaxation and escape from the day's stress.

#5—The Dictatorship Leader

This leader has a thing for deadlines and has the attitude that your work should be your life. He cannot understand that people have lives outside of work, and he wants everyone to know he is in charge. Often, the dictatorial leader will work weekends and holidays and will let you know it. People that disagree with the dictatorial leader will either never be heard from again, as their careers are quickly cut short with the company, or they will be overloaded with demeaning tasks and projects well below their abilities.

#6—The Leader of None

This type of leader is unhappy and lonely. He has become team leader by default, because he is the last member of the team. He has been doing the same job for many years and does a great job. The company does not want to lose him because he has become irreplaceable, and it would be difficult to find someone that would do the same job for such a low salary. Therefore, in an effort to keep him, management has promoted him to team manager or manager of some one-man department of which he is the only employee.

#7—The Best Friend Leader

The best friend type leader wants to please everyone at all times. He has no clue that pleasing everyone is next to impossible, and as a result, everyone hates him, yet he has no clue as to why he is hated. His frustration comes from the fact that he is busy trying to please the boss, which upsets the team, but when he tries to please the team, the boss accuses him of not communicating. This is because he tries to sugarcoat bad news in both directions so that he is never perceived as the bearer of bad news.

#8—The Reluctant Leader

The reluctant leader generally volunteers for the position because no one else wants the position, including himself. Nevertheless, in the best interest of the team, he reluctantly assumes the position, because management has decided that every team must have a leader. Other times, management appoints or promotes the reluctant leader to the position simply because they feel he needs a challenge and will not achieve his full potential otherwise.

#9—The Puppet Leader

This type of leader is intelligent, but a scheming and manipulative boss has led him astray. His boss has drawn him into various schemes to further the boss's agenda. This type of leader is easily diverted and is easily cornered when things go wrong. He quickly becomes the boss's scapegoat. The puppet leader can be fun to work for, but is not outside the possibility of going off the deep end and lashing out when you least expect it.

#10—The Serious Leader

The serious leader runs a tight ship. He will not put up with socializing or extended breaks and is an avid clock-watcher. He is quick to break up gatherings in the office kitchen by reminding team members of their project deadlines. He will often give a quick lecture on how congregating in the kitchen sets a poor example for other employees when in actuality, he is more concerned that his boss will view him as not having his team under control.

#11—The In-over-his-head Leader

This leader wants to do the right thing and feels an obligation to the company to do a good job as team leader, but he is simply in over his head.

His knowledge far exceeds his abilities, and generally, he has been promoted based on his seniority rather than his ability to handle the position. Many times, these leaders know they have been promoted beyond their ability, but they will hang onto the position, knowing they will never be able to get another job at that level.

#12—The Political Leader

Generally appointed to the position by upper management, the political leader has a clear agenda based on what management has described as the "problem." This leader is not interested in furthering the team or building a more efficient work environment that can handle growth and cultivate new ideas. He is interested in cutting costs and figuring out how to do the same job with fewer people and less money. His position is clearly political in nature, and he knows that once he has completed his task, he is out of there.

The political leader is generally an outside consultant that management has contracted to solve a problem. The problem is that once he has collected his paycheck and slashed spending, he does not have to stick around and wait for the consequences of his decisions. When the department or team fails, management is quick to blame the remaining team members for not following through on the consultant's plans.

What is the Perfect Team Leader?

I am sure that as you read the profiles of the various team leader types I identified here, your mind drifted back to thoughts of some managers you may have dealt with in the past. In fact, you may even be able to place that past team leader into two or more classifications, demonstrating that a team leader's personality cannot be concretely defined.

There is no set formula for the perfect team leader, as each team is different because teams are comprised of individuals working toward a common goal. The individual personalities that a team leader will be working with will vary from person to person. What worked for the team leader with one team member may not work with a different team member.

What the best team leaders have in common is their set of values, loyalty to the company, and loyalty to their teams—in that order. At the core is their set of values, a set of values that are inflexible. Beyond their values is their loyalty to the company—not a blind loyalty, but a well placed loyalty that conforms to their personal values. If something in the company does violate their personal values, they are quick to correct the company rather than shift their values.

The perfect leader would rather resign from the company than ignore his values. These leaders have integrity, which they often demonstrate by showing their loyalty to their teams by extending and combining their values with those of their team members.

It should also be noted that a great team leader might demonstrate some of the characteristics described above. The primary difference is that the great team leader has the ability to pick and choose which traits he wishes to demonstrate based on the situation, as long as the traits he demonstrates do not conflict with his values, the company values, or the team's values.

Values

Values are those things that matter to each of us—the ideas and beliefs we hold as special. Treating others with respect, for example, is a value, as is keeping a promise. Most of us learned our values or morals, if you prefer, from religious organizations, school, parents, and organizations such as the Boy Scouts or Girl Scouts.

So what role do your values play in leading your team? Frankly, they are essential in creating a team with a can-do attitude—a team that can handle the most demanding projects. However, if your values are not in line with the can-do attitude you want from your team, then you have a long difficult journey ahead.

Values are not something that you can assign to your team. You cannot simply state that showing up on time for work is a value that the team should respect. You make rules, not values. If you do not value showing up to work on time, are constantly late for meetings, or take extended lunches whenever you please, then punctuality is not a value to you, and your team will adopt a similar attitude toward punctuality. They too will be late for work and meetings. When you try to enforce the rules of punctuality, you will be viewed as a hypocrite and lose credibility.

However, if you show up to work early, are the first one in the conference room, and adhere to company policy, you will find that your team will emulate your punctuality. Punctuality is not the only value that your team will emulate, however. Your team will quickly learn what values you have and will emulate them, good or bad.

If you value the opinions of other team members, then team members will also value the opinions of other team members. However, if you appear to disregard other members' views or ideas and only promote your ideas, then your team will become fractured, and members will discount other ideas while promoting their own.

Many times, I have witnessed team leaders openly show disrespect for managers and team leaders of other departments. They will openly inform their team members, "So-and-so has no idea what he is talking about." These same team leaders are dumbfounded when they discover a member of their own team talking behind their backs making statements such as, "So-and-so has no idea how to manage a team." These managers are oblivious as to why their team members would do such a thing. The truth is, their team members are simply mimicking the behavior the manager has established by talking poorly about other managers.

So how do we create a set of values for the team? Team values are the intrinsic qualities and beliefs that a group of employees puts forward as a team. They sit at the top of the pyramid of leadership levels.

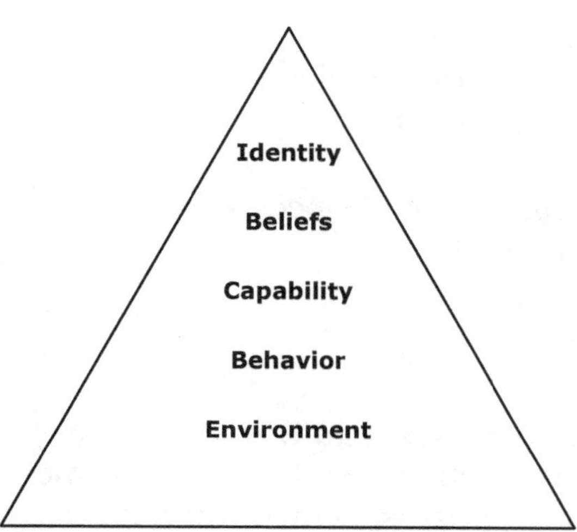

Once formulated, team values, together with the team vision and mission statement, will shape the team's identity. These values can be shared with customers and other staff members. Your team's values may even help attract new staff members or customers. They show what you believe in.

As stated earlier, values are not created, but are simply recognized or extracted from the company's values as well as the values of the team leaders. This is why it is difficult to document your team's values as well as the company's values.

Values should be formulated in an honest and truthful fashion, and they will involve consulting the team members as well as the top management. Some typical values that many organizations recognize as core values are:

- Quality
- Leadership
- Passion for Excellence
- Accountability
- Trust
- Integrity and Respect
- Teamwork
- Creativity

The key is to design a list of which everybody shares the same values, otherwise the list of values becomes too general and meaningless. Once you have set a list of about ten core values, you will need to detail each one by explaining why these are the values for which you stand.

For example, if *accountability* is one of your core values, then you may formulate what *accountability* means as follows:

- Be accountable for one's actions.

- Empower yourself to do what is right for the customer.

The important part in establishing your team's core values is that everyone must share the same values, and you, as team leader, must live by those values.

In today's world, most companies establish rules and treat them with legal compliance, stating all employees must obey the rules. These companies are satisfied with the status quo. These organizations simply survive. Then there are those companies that have adopted ethical values at the core of how they manage the company. These organizations are flourishing even during difficult economic times. These companies understand that core values add value to their products and services.

To paraphrase Albert Einstein: Try not to become a man of rules, but rather try to become a man of values. Rules can be bent, broken, or ignored; values are inflexible and enduring.

Essentials for Guiding Excellence

I recently read a great book by Joe Vitale called *Buying Trances.* In one particular section, Joe Vitale talks about a marketing genius named Roy Garn. I was so intrigued with Joe's writing about Garn that I had to do some more research on him.

Garn had identified four basic elements that identify the various mental states that preoccupy nearly everyone's thoughts. They are

- Self-preservation
- Romance
- Money
- Recognition

After looking into these four basic mental states, it occurred to me that they are not simply marketing related, but life related, and even job related. These four simple elements are the keys to guiding excellence for your team. Granted, they may not appear to be job related at first glance, but the underlying emotion of each is what concerns each employee, each team member, and each person within the organization.

Let's adjust each of these elements a little so that they are more in line with your team. Below is a translated list that better represents each of these elements as they relate to your team.

1. Job Security
2. Motivation
3. Money
4. Self-esteem

By having a complete understanding of how these mental preoccupations affect your team, you will be better able to understand and provide the excellent leadership your team deserves.

Job security

Every employee wants job security, but very few employees have it these days. Job security, or better described as "job insecurity," eats away at the mental health of your team members, creating doubt and causing team members to second-guess and overanalyze nearly everything they do. An employee that is afraid he may lose his job does not want to make any mistakes for fear of being terminated, and as a result, he creates a self-full-filling prophecy.

He becomes so preoccupied making sure he does not make a mistake that he ends up making mistakes, and usually, they are big ones because his mind is generally not on the task. The result is he makes too many mistakes, and he is terminated, fulfilling the prophecy and reassuring his beliefs, as well as everyone else's belief, that mistakes can get you fired. As a result, the feelings of insecurity spread.

Motivation

Productive employees need motivation. You cannot get quality work out of an employee that is not motivated to do so. The best motivation comes from within the employees themselves. The passion keeps them going, moving on against all odds. As both a computer programmer and a writer, I can attest to the fact that the most creative moments in my career have not been because of motivation induced by my employer, but from within—my own determination to solve a problem, explain a point of view, or become an expert in something about which I previously knew nothing. My own thirst for knowledge and understanding drives me.

Each of us has within, a force that drives us, that interests us, that pushes us to continue when others would stop. As the team leader, you must find what drives your team members and then provide the fuel they need to keep their fires burning.

Money

What can I say about money other than everyone wants as much as they can possibly get their hands on. Unless your team is comprised of volunteers, money is what is used to compensate your team members for their time and efforts.

Money is a tool that allows your team members to pay their bills, nothing more. You cannot dangle it in front of them as a carrot in the hope of motivating them. It is not something you can threaten them with if they do not perform. It is compensation for their efforts.

Yes, it is possible their efforts will not be up to your standards, or they may not produce the desired results, but it should never be used as a reward or as a punishment. If you use money as a punishment, you will quickly find job security, motivation, and self-esteem quickly dissolve as they are directly linked with money.

Self-esteem

Everyone needs self-esteem. People need to be wanted, to have value, and add value. Self-esteem is, in my opinion, the most powerful of the four essentials of guiding excellence. Self-esteem has the power to create motivation where there was no motivation, to create passion where once there was none. I have seen self-esteem completely transform an employee that was at the end of the proverbial rope into an incredible team leader.

If an employee has low self-esteem, that employee will not be motivated to work at his best. He will not have the passion you need your team members to have in order to solve problems or complete projects on time. Do all you can to build self-esteem in your team, and you will see incredible transformations take place in each team member as well as the team itself.

Do all you can for your team. Treat them fairly, pay them a fair wage, build their self-esteem, feed the fires of their passions, and treat them as the valuable team members that they are, and you will see miraculous things happen within your team.

Attitude Is Everything

What is attitude and how can your attitude influence your success at work? Learning successful attitude skills will help resolve and defuse many potentially problematic situations. Attitude is a set way of thinking that affects everything you do, including your work, productivity, relationships, and your success. Many think attitude is an emotion that only they can feel. The reality is that your attitude is visible to other people through your behavior and is reflected in your job.

Most people are unaware of the triggers that cause their attitude. The good news is that attitude can be changed. If you already have a great attitude, you can improve upon it and hone it for maximum success. As you improve your attitude, you will discover a domino effect that will positively affect all aspects of your life. Your attitude is your own. It defines you, the world's perception of you, and ultimately, your success at work, in relationships, and in life in general.

A positive attitude can also be contagious. It can establish the tone of meetings before anyone even opens his mouth to begin the meeting. How many meetings have you been to where there was a negative overtone before the meeting even started? You simply knew in advance who called the meeting, and you were familiar with his attitude. Therefore, you knew the meeting was going to be difficult. This is usually the case in organizations where employees are treated as indentured servants rather than valuable assets.

Negative attitude brings down morale, productivity, and profits. Unfortunately, negative attitudes are an unpleasant fact, and you will have to deal with them, but you do not have to have one. I cannot think of a single business or personal success that resulted from a negative attitude. If you can think of one, I would be willing to bet that, upon closer examination, someone involved had a positive attitude, and he is the one that is responsible for the successes. "The greatest discovery of any generation is that a human being can alter his life by altering his attitude."—William James.

A Touch of Class

Maybe you heard it growing up: "Sit up straight," "Don't drag your feet," "Don't chew with your mouth open," or "Tuck your shirt in," and you rolled your eyes and begrudgingly did as you were told. Unbelievably, these are all valuable lessons for success.

We have all heard the old adage, "Don't judge a book by its cover." The reality is that people do judge the book by the cover. The cover is the first thing we see when selecting a book. The only way to determine if the book is any good is to read it. Your appearance is the same as that book cover, and people will judge you on your appearance.

I am sure that at some time in your life, you have listened to someone on the radio, and based on the sound of his voice, you created a mental image of what that person on the radio looked like. You may have envisioned a tall, middle-aged gentleman, well dressed and clean shaven—only to have your mental image shattered when you saw the person on a television interview. To your amazement, you found out that the person was a short, stocky guy with clothing that looked as if he fell asleep on the sofa.

The same is true of your image. People will naturally create a mental image of your professionalism, intelligence, and character based on what you look like. Claude M. Bristol once said, "Every person is the creation of himself, the image of his own thinking and believing. As individuals think and believe, so they are."

"You only get the chance to make a first impression once" is a profound statement. Whether it is a new job interview, a meeting with your boss, or a presentation to the board of directors, the mental images that people create upon meeting you will determine how successful you will be in dealing with that person. It does not matter whether you are meeting them for the first time or the one-hundredth time, your appearance will determine how other people perceive you at that moment.

Imagine yourself sitting in an office waiting room waiting for a job interview. Across from you is a well-dressed James Bond-type gentleman— well groomed, confident, and obviously dressed for success. You have the experience, the knowledge to perform the job at hand—you are a perfect fit for the job. You have your résumé in order, you are well organized, and you have the credentials to back up your experience. You are calm; you fear nothing!

You sit calmly as the other candidate is escorted into his interview. Ten minutes, twenty minutes, finally, an hour passes, and he emerges from his interview and confidently exits the reception area. Your name is called! You stand up and walk into the office for your interview. You are offered a chair, and you sit down, only to realize you are facing the interviewer. Directly behind her is a huge mirror, and you suddenly notice that you have mismatched shoes, your shirt looks like you slept in it, and your pants have a hole in the knee.

At this point, where do you think your confidence level is? By this point, it really does not matter what you say, the odds are the interviewer has made up her mind before you even opened your mouth. Her mental image of your personality has been established in her mind's eye. At this point, however, not all is lost! You can still save the interview with your experience, knowledge, and skills, but it will not be easy. You still have to convince the interviewer to reject the mental image her mind's eye has created of your abilities.

To paraphrase P. J. O'Rourke, the more extraordinary you are, the more dignified you should look. It also works in reverse. When I see a kid with three or four rings in his nose, I know there is nothing extraordinary about that person.

Your appearance can make you or break you. If you want to succeed in business or life in general, you need to establish the right mindsets, both yours and everyone else's. You may be thinking it is not fair to judge someone by the way they dress, but the reality is, life is not fair. People will naturally assume that how things look on the outside is an indication of how things are on the inside. American historian Christopher Lasch summed it up best when he said, "Nothing succeeds like the appearance of success."

Etiquette

We previously discussed proper clothing and that your appearance is the first thing a person sees as you enter a room. We also discussed how people have a tendency to draw conclusions based on your appearance. Assuming you are now properly dressed and have created a positive visual first impression, we can move on to your actions. After all, what good is dressing well and creating the proper image if your mannerisms are that of a scavenger foraging for food.

One of the most common meeting venues in business today is the business lunch or dinner. It is a shame that so many bright managers and up-and-coming employees do not have a proper understanding of dining etiquette.

I cannot imagine, for a moment, Donald Trump licking his fingers after consuming a dinner roll, while at the same time discussing a multi-million dollar deal over lunch, or Warren Buffet meeting Bill Gates for dinner and greeting him with a weak, limp-wristed handshake.

Let's get to work on improving your dining etiquette, so that you can complement your pristine physical appearance with manners that speak volumes about your character. Presented here are some suggestions by Mercedes Alfaro, CEO of First Impression Management, an etiquette and professional image management company, for those meeting while dining out:

- When at the table, the bread plate on the left is yours; the water glass on the right is yours.
- The napkin goes in your lap when you sit down or when the host puts his in his lap.
- The napkin goes into your lap with the fold forward, away from your torso.
- It is a napkin, not a washcloth; use it to wipe your fingers or mouth. Anything more requires a trip to the restroom.
- It is a napkin, not a tissue; no blowing your nose, in fact, no nose blowing at the table ever.
- If you need to clean yourself, go to the restroom. That includes cleaning spills from your clothes.
- Pass things such as the breadbasket and condiments before you help yourself.
- If you are the host, you pay for the meal, period.
- If you are concerned about wrestling for the bill, arrive early and give your credit card to the wait

staff with instructions to bring the receipt to you at the conclusion of the meal.

- When seated, the person of highest importance gets the best seat at the table—the one with the best view.
- The person inviting another to a meal should recommend a restaurant, trying to discover food preferences ahead of the invitation when possible.
- Cell phones should be off or on vibrate—no answering, text messaging, or calling during the meal.
- Never hold your fork like a dagger with the tines coming out the bottom of your hand. It should rest in the palm of your hand, the tines coming out between the thumb and forefinger. When the hand is closed and turned palm down, the curved back of the fork should rest just under your index finger.
- Do not use your knife as a saw. Use easy stroking motions, drawing the handle toward yours. If you are having difficulty, ask for a sharper knife.
- Official etiquette rules state no business until the entrée dishes are cleared away. This is unfortunately not practical in most cases, as you may have limited time, particularly at lunch.
- A rule of thumb is to spend about one-third of the meal discussing non-business issues, one-third discussing business, and the final third away from business again. Then, at the conclusion of the meal, recap the steps that each will take.

- Develop a good handshake. The pattern is palm-to-palm, web-of-thumb to web-of-thumb, and fingers wrapped around the other person's hand. Pump up and down two to three times; this applies equally to men and women.

- While, very traditionally, it remains good manners for a man to stand up when a woman arrives at or leaves the table, it is no longer a requirement, particularly in a business environment.

- If there is an issue with food or the bill, do not address it at the table. Excuse yourself and talk to the wait staff or manager as appropriate.

- Remember that not everyone has good manners or etiquette, but they nearly always recognize it.

Your actions and mannerisms are the second thing after your physical appearance that people will use to pass judgment upon you. How you present yourself is just as important as how you dress. When you dress appropriately, speak eloquently, and display proper etiquette, you are positioning yourself as someone that is trustworthy and considerate.

Whether you are having a business meal with your team members, your manager, or a client, the impression you make based on your appearance and the etiquette you demonstrate will be long remembered after that meal. Do not waste that lasting impression by leaving your associates with the image of an ill-mannered slob. If you do, odds are they will remember you, but not in the way that you want or in a way that advances your career.

To expand on a comment made by Clarence Thomas, Associate Justice of the United States Supreme Court: good manners will open doors that the best education cannot, but poor manners can slam doors shut that took years of education to open.

Build Staff Capacity

To build staff capacity, you must be a good leader, and to be a good leader, you must make yourself replaceable. I know that this goes against the popular concept of making yourself indispensable, so you cannot be replaced. However, the truth is that everyone can be replaced; it is just a matter of how difficult the task is of replacing you.

The idea in building staff capacity is to make yourself indispensable because you are a valuable employee, not because replacing you would be a hassle. John Maxwell, author of *The 21 Irrefutable Laws of Leadership*, explains it this way:

> *The only way to make yourself indispensable is to make yourself dispensable. In other words, if you are able to continually empower others and help them develop so that they become capable of taking over your job, you will become so valuable to the organization that you become indispensable.*

To make yourself dispensable, you will need to learn to delegate tasks to other team members. Train various team members to perform tasks that you normally would do and have them continue to perform those tasks and provide you with a status report. If it is not possible for them to continue to perform the tasks on an ongoing basis, then at least have them perform them occasionally as a refresher.

As time progresses, you will find that you will have more time to pursue other tasks that require your attention as your team deals with day-to-day tasks. Eventually, you may begin to assign one or two team members supervisory responsibility for other tasks that the team performs. Before you do this, however, take them aside and inform them as to why you are assigning additional tasks to them. Not doing so could be interpreted as you unfairly singling them out for additional work. Make them aware that you are grooming them for a managerial position sometime in the future. This will go a long way towards motivating them to perform at their peak as you have shown the confidence in their abilities.

As Stephen Covey puts it in habit two of his *The 7 Habits of Highly Effective People*, "Begin with the end in mind." In this case, the result is to build a team that has the skills and knowledge to handle any situation that should occur. This builds confidence in the team and, in turn, makes you more valuable to the organization.

The idea behind building staff capacity is not to dominate knowledge, but to distribute it to as many team members as possible. The more information and knowledge of other jobs your team has, the better they can perform their own jobs.

Background of Your Team

Who are your team members? Sounds like an easy question, but in reality, many managers cannot get beyond their team members' names when asked this question. The *who* I am asking about is a much more complex question. When I ask, "Who are your team members?" I want to *know* who they are. What are their likes and dislikes? What are their hobbies? What makes them tick? What drives them?

These are the answers you should know to answer the question, "Who are your team members?" Why? Because all those dynamics are brought to your team. They make up not just the souls of the individual team members, but they are the soul of your team.

Early in my career, I had a team of programmers, and all I really knew about them were their names. Sure, I knew other things about them, such as the food they preferred, how they liked their coffee, and a thousand other little things about them, but I did not *know* them.

It was not until I sat down and spoke with each member of the team and had a real conversation with him, about him. You know the type of conversation about which I am talking. I am talking about the type where you interact with each other, your comments are relevant to the subject matter being discussed, and you actually listen to each other.

It was during one of these conversations that I learned that one of my programmers was once a CPA and worked for a bank. Another team member had a knack for statistics, while another team member enjoyed solving complex puzzles. Once I had found out this new information about my team, things started to make sense as to why projects were taking longer than they should, why applications were plagued with bugs. I had the wrong team members working on the wrong software. I had the puzzle solver writing accounting interfaces, the CPA writing reports, and the statistician developing data entry systems.

My team members were out of their element with the tasks I had assigned them. As a result, they were unsure of themselves, constantly discussing with other team members how they would handle the issues, and then they would try their best to get the job done.

It was at that point I held a team meeting to discuss project assignments. I discussed my findings with each of them. The CPA, for example, had informed me that he hated accounting, and that is why he moved into programming. Therefore, to respect his views, we discussed the matter, and he agreed to become the team's point man on all accounting issues, but he was not assigned all the accounting projects. This resulted in better team organization, mentoring, and the exchange of knowledge. The CPA was able to work on the projects he found interesting while at the same time helping those team members that needed accounting help. If an accounting issue arose, he was our pinch hitter.

All this exemplifies the need to *know* your team's background. By knowing your team's strengths, weaknesses, pet peeves, and passions, you will be able to assign tasks better as well as understand the point of view your team members may have on an issue. Each of your team members has his unique abilities, views, and opinions. Because of these various views, your team is unique in every aspect, and it is your responsibility to the company to use that uniqueness.

It is for this reason that I feel the term *genius* is the correct term when dealing with teams. Each team member offers a new perspective to the project, bringing his own genius to the team. The word *genius* as defined by the *American Heritage Dictionary* is

> *A genius is a person with distinguished mental prowess. This can manifest either as a foremost intellect, or as an outstanding creative talent. The term genius specifically applies to mental rather than athletic skills.*

Based on this definition, and the fact that each member of your team is a member because he offers some sort of value to the team, whether it is intellect, creativity, or some other distinguishing trait, your team is comprised of *geniuses.* Your Guiding Genius will determine whether the team is just an ordinary team or an outstanding team.

Why Teams

Every industry has its giants, its super achiever, and its genius. Microsoft has Bill Gates, Google has Larry Page and Sergey Brin, and Chrysler Corporation had Lee A. Iacocca. How did these people build such successful companies? Was it by chance and dumb luck? Did they rule with an iron fist? The answer to these questions is NO!

Their success and the success of the businesses are due to their determination and understanding of the people behind the business—the employees! Employees are the lifeblood of any organization. A team of strong employees can fuel a strong company and build upon its own strengths.

The secret then is how these geniuses of industry built those winning teams. Well, just as your body needs nourishment and vitamins and minerals to perform at its peak, so do the employees. To employees, fair treatment, encouragement, and self-esteem are the nutrients they need to perform the tasks they are assigned.

Imagine what you could accomplish with your team if you knew how captains of industry such as Warren Buffet of Berkshire Hathaway, Ray Kroc of McDonald's, or even Microsoft's Bill Gates were able to motivate their teams to produce the results that have made these corporations the successes they are today.

Well, the truth is, these industry giants treat their teams with respect. They understand that the team makes things happen. Ray Kroc created the vision of what McDonald's could be, but the team he built made it a reality. Bill Gates created the vision that is Windows and continues to forge new visions, and then he lets his team turn those visions into reality. As the team leader, it is your responsibility to insure that your team shares the same vision and works toward the same goal. But what if you do not have a team? What if you are the team?

Well, you would first create a list of all the things that need to be done on a project. Next, you would begin working on that project, one item at a time. About halfway through the first item, you start to realize there is more to do, so you start adding to your list. Quickly, you become overwhelmed with projects to complete. You find yourself jumping from one project to another. You are working hard, you are completing many tasks, but not a single project is being completed.

You quickly realize that you need help. Two or three more people working on these tasks could get your projects completed in a reasonable amount of time. Therefore, you hire a few others to help. Suddenly, they are looking to you for guidance. Guess what? You have a team.

Teams are a natural progression of business in today's business world. If you want productivity, you will need a team. Teams motivate each other to perform more work in less time than an individual could perform in the same amount of time. In the end, a team can also do the job for less money as well.

An example would be building a house. Can a single person build a house? Sure, many have done it. However, it can take a long time on your own. It all boils down to hours, or *person-hours*. If building a house will take 14,000 person-hours to build, then a single person working eight hours per day, seven days a week can complete that house in approximately five years. However, when you put a team of fifteen workers on that same house, working eight hours a day, seven days a week, then the house will be completed in approximately four months.

Teamwork is how business is done. You can even find teamwork in the smallest of businesses, including the one-man operation. Vendors, suppliers, and even clients can all be team members. So, remember, as Lee Iacocca once said,

"In the end, all business operations can be reduced to three words: people, product, and profits. Unless you've got a good team, you can't do much with the other two."

Get to Know Your Team

As a team leader, you will be working with several different personalities, each with his particular way of doing things, understanding situations, and handling stress. You will be relying on these team members to get things done just as any team working on a project is expected to. The problem is not all team members are cut from the same cloth, so to speak. They all have unique abilities, expertise, and skills, which is why they are on your team in the first place. Their talents provide your team with the diverse points of view they need to get the job done.

Your team may consist of bookkeepers, accountants, auditors, and collections specialists, or it may consist of network administrators, programmers, database administrators, and support specialists, to name just a few. The multitudes of combinations of talent on any particular team are like snowflakes—no two are alike.

Some team members are easier to work with than others are. Some will take responsibility easily; others will avoid it all together. Some employees may want to be involved in everything but may not be qualified, and yet others have their own agenda.

Nearly all team members can be classified into one of the following categories. Each category has its own pros and cons in regards to the projects you need to assign. It is important to understand that this type of classification does not indicate the value of a team member, but rather acts as a method for determining the tactics required to deal with each type of team member. So with that said, let's take a look at your team members:

Over loaders

Over loaders are quick to volunteer for new projects or tasks and are generally capable of performing the requested duties. However, these team members may have time management issues. These team members generally get bored with a task or project quickly once the novelty wears off.

You will need to help these team members better utilize their time and add enough of a challenge to keep the tasks interesting. You may need to establish guidelines for requesting new projects before old projects are completed.

Ladder climbers

Ladder climbers are self-serving, and they will seek out high profile projects simply for the notoriety and the ability for self-promotion. They are not interested in the team, but they will quickly point the finger when something goes wrong, rather than being accountable for their errors or miscalculations in judgment.

These team members have delicate egos and quickly become defensive when approached regarding an issue. They will need to be handled tactfully and cautiously, yet firmly. These team members can usually handle whatever they volunteer for, as they are cautious not to volunteer for tasks or projects that may place a negative spotlight on them. Because of their need for recognition, employee appreciation awards, fringe benefits, and small tokens of appreciation go a long way in motivating them to perform many tasks.

Eager but unable

These team members cannot perform the tasks they have volunteered to perform. They are well intentioned, and they want to perform but just do not have the skills required to perform the tasks. They usually refuse any offer of assistance as they view it as weakness and do not want to give the impression they have gotten in over their heads. As a result, the task either will not be done or will be so poorly done that it will have to be redone by a more qualified team member.

These team members desperately want to be needed, and they want to please. Assign them tasks that are within their skill set and gradually increase the difficulty of the tasks as their skills improve. You may also want to create tasks that are geared toward training where they have the opportunity to assist a more skilled team member with a clearly defined chain of authority for the task. This will help them develop the skills they require to handle tasks on their own while becoming accustomed to working with other team members.

Resistant

A resistant team member is not a bad team member. These team members do not like change and assigning them a new task is a change that makes them uncomfortable. They do not volunteer for tasks and do not take responsibility for their actions or inactions. They may point the finger at other team members or you, as the team leader, with an "I told you so" attitude.

This team member's resistance often stems from a lack of confidence or understanding of the requirements of the task, as well as low self-esteem. In many cases, lack of knowledge is the most cited cause of resistance in accepting additional responsibility.

You will need to build his self-esteem and confidence in his own ability to perform assigned tasks. Assign new tasks gradually, starting with small easily performed tasks to help build self-esteem and get them used to accepting additional tasks.

Untrained but willing

Most team members will fall into this category unless they are highly trained or have been with the company for a long time. They are willing to perform new tasks but simply do not have the knowledge to perform the task.

These team members are willing to learn and accept training and mentoring well. They will need guidance to perform the assigned task and may make mistakes. This is normal and is not a sign of incompetence; they simply need training. Eventually, these team members become ideal team members provided they get the training and encouragement they need.

Ideal

The ideal team member is just that—ideal. They are happy to accept new projects and as much responsibility as you can assign. They accept input from others well and follow through on commitments. They have no problem asking for help. These team members require little to no monitoring, and they should be rewarded often for their dedication and skills. Keep an eye out for these employees. They can be ideal candidates for training and mentoring others, as well as candidates for promotion, should the opportunity arise.

The best part of having a team is that you can share the workload with your team. It is important, however, to understand each of your team members' skills and abilities as well as his desires for advancement when assigning tasks.

Learn who your team is, what they want from the job, what their goals are, and where they see themselves in two years, five years, or even ten years. Then work with them to achieve those goals.

Guiding vs. Leading

Many people do not see the difference between guiding and leading. They fail to understand the nuances of these two strategies in management. You may be wondering the exact same thing at this point, so let's get started.

As we discussed earlier, your team is comprised of geniuses that bring unique perspectives to the team. The last thing you want to do at this point is de-motivate, discourage, or devalue the team in any way. In order to maintain your team's perspective, you first need to understand how the team members became the valuable intellectual assets they are. They did it by thinking, by being themselves, by blazing their own paths. Geniuses are not followers. They are self-motivated, independent thinking individuals who need your guidance.

To force your team members into a leader/follower environment will destroy the creative process that is so important to the success of the team. In order to lead a team of *geniuses*, you would need to eliminate independent thinking, force conformity, and turn your team of geniuses into unhappy, resentful followers.

A quick check of the dictionary points out many interesting things about *lead* as a verb, for example, "to direct the operations, activity, or performance of," such as in the case of an attorney in court that leads the witness, or "to guide a dance partner through the steps of a dance." As you can see, leading implies that someone will perform a task in accordance with a predetermined result. Another interesting note was this reference in the Merriam-Webster Dictionary, "LEAD implies showing the way and often keeping those that follow under control and in order."

Unfortunately, *leading* is how many managers deal with their teams. They force them to fit the corporate image and try to lead them by controlling them. They then wonder why production and morale drop and then constantly change policy and tactics in a futile attempt to achieve the unachievable.

The name of this book is *Your Guiding Genius* and for good reason. Guiding encourages the team to make their decisions. The Merriam-Webster Dictionary has this to say, "GUIDE implies intimate knowledge of the way and of all its difficulties and dangers." Your job is to guide your team in the direction you want, but your team needs to select their path to that result. Only through guidance, will your team learn and expand their knowledge, which in turn increases the value of the team as a collective.

As a team *leader*, it is important not to confuse your position as a leader to mean *lead*. Team leader is simply another title that business has bestowed on you to indicate that you are in charge of a team. It is up to you to choose how to manage your team. You can either lead a team of mindless followers or guide a team of geniuses that will make you invaluable.

Office Politics

Every office dynamic has politics! If someone tells you they once worked at a company that had no politics, then it is safe to say they were lying, do not know what office politics are, and/or the company has gone out of business.

Politics is the method used to resolve problems within many organizations. The key is keeping those politics positively motivated. When a team sits down and determines what projects are to have a particular priority— that is politics!

Politics is the process by which collective decisions are made within groups. Although the term generally applies to negative behavior within companies, politics is observed in all human group interactions.

Jim Dustin, a friend of mine from a large national health insurance company, stated it best in an e-mail exchange we had regarding this subject. He stated

> *Office politics run the full gamut from positive behavior of team leaders and individual employees who continue to improve customer satisfaction, to negative behaviors driven by insecure employees seeking self-importance and personal rewards and advancement with no regard for those on the ladder to success.*
>
> *The one common thread I see is that it in any office, from the giant corporation to a small office setting, the phenomena needs to be acknowledged with awareness.*
>
> *Can businesses do without office politics? I'd say with the right environment we can*

manage it to become a business advantage. The negative behavior is of course useless.

If the office environment is poisoned beyond repair, if a senior leadership structure has allowed negative behavior to exist and flourish, then the company could be reaching its downward turn, and the disease is too embedded for the company to survive without radical surgery—if at all.

The negative aspects of office politics are legendary. Scott Adams' cartoon script Dilbert is a humorous reflection of management absurdities, and Mike Judge's Office Space, the movie, distributed by 20th Century Fox, should probably be used by learning and organizational development consultants as an example of how not to manage people.

Smart leaders are aware of how important actively inspiring, setting tone, creating a vision, framing attitude, and enabling ideas to develop into products and services is what they are supposed to do. It is their top priority to "walk the talk" and carefully monitor that their reports all the way down the chain are equally motivated and engaged. This is about ecosystems where positive reinforcement at every level, from peer-to-peer to a "pat on the back" from the manager—all coordinate to create a healthy organism.

This behavior can be trained to cross over functional boundaries of departments, and if managed with awareness, can make a company's value soar and its people inspired and proud to contribute.

Nature hates a vacuum, so in the absence of this kind of positive, merit based, congenial environment—is when the bullies find victims, gossip replaces fact, aggressive ambition trumps risk management and on and on.

I submit that it's about leadership and creating an office culture that systematically eradicates the negative components. How that gets achieved can be customized in each setting—and ultimately becomes as important to get right as any of the actual "work" being done.

What most people mistake as politics are actually the actions of select individuals with personal agendas that use the political process within a business for their own personal advancement with no consideration for their fellow employees. Generally, when an office environment is experiencing negative *politics*, the reality is that the office environment lacks a political structure to regulate the decision process properly. This is usually a result of weak leadership, poor planning, poor communications, or a combination of these elements.

A manager who says, "I'm not political" is in great danger. Only those that acknowledge and embrace office politics will survive, and the successful manager will be the one who understands his office's politics and can use that political process in a positive way to advance his teams and ultimately the company's goals rather than his own personal agenda.

The Generation Gap

C. S. Lewis once said, "You are never too old to set another goal or to dream a new dream." Loosely translated, it means you are never too old to learn something new. However, in today's fast-paced business world, the newest generations are quickly entering the work force with their ideas on how to network, market, and run a business. Yet, they should realize—no matter how much you think you know, you can still learn more.

We are all part of a new-age experiment—four generations working side by side yet often speaking a different language. Think that is an exaggeration? Go ahead. Try to decipher this twenty-something text message: WU CMIW that was CLM or maybe CS. Loosely translated, it says, "What's up? Correct me if I'm wrong. That was a career-limiting move or maybe career suicide."

Nearly fifty million Americans were born in the Silent Generation between 1925 through 1945. Today about 95 percent of the Silent Generation is retired. In a few short years, virtually no Silent Generation members will be in command of industry, a battlefield, or anything else for that matter. And with them will go generations of experience, knowledge, and know-how.

Born of the Get-it-done (G. I.) Generation, the Silent Generation followed the Get-it-done G.I.'s and grew up expecting disappointment but still had faith in whatever they did. They did not question authority; they respected it and did as they were told. They expected to work at one company their entire lives and retire.

After World War II, birth rates soared. These children born between 1946 and 1964 grew up under the influence of the G.I. and Silent Generations. They have a strong work ethic, they ask questions to understand better what is expected of them, and they participate well with coworkers. They are the Baby Boomers.

Baby Boomers are realists. They organize life around work, not work around life. They realize they must work their way to the top, and only hard work and determination will get them there. They have the attitude, "If you're unhappy in a relationship, then exit it," and "If you don't like your job, find a different one." Their jobs and status symbols are important to them.

Born of the early Baby Boomers between 1965 and 1982 is Generation "X." This generation is also known as the 13th Generation, because it is the 13th generation to know the flag of the United States, counting back to the peers of Benjamin Franklin, as explained in the book *Generations* by William Strauss and Neil Howe.

Generation "X" is disaffectionate with government and lacks trust of any leadership. This generation has had an increase in educational variation, as it has witnessed the end of the Cold War. They grew up in a world of increased divorce rates, rampant political apathy, and the zero population growth movement where children were something you took a pill not to have.

Finally is Generation "Y," born between 1983 and 1997. Generation "Y" is also known as the "Net Generation." Born into a world of high tech, today 95 percent own a computer and cell phone; 76 percent use instant messaging and text messaging to communicate; 49 percent download music instantly; and 75 percent have a page on Facebook.com or MySpace.com. This is a connected generation.

Generation "Y" wants instant gratification: instant music, video on demand, instant access to friends and information from their Blackberry cell phones and bluetooth headset. This generation tends to charge in where others are cautious. Generation "Y" has fewer marketable skills; they are demanding, impatient, and far from being loyal. Poor spelling, grammar, and failure to understand what constitutes appropriate corporate behavior are some of the shortfalls of Generation "Y."

With all these different attitudes coming together in business today, nearly 60 percent of HR managers at large companies say they have observed office conflicts that flow from generational differences, according to the Society for Human Resource Management. In nearly all cases of office tension, communications has been cited as the most significant factor in bridging the generation gap.

Team leaders would be wise to stress communications and respect within its multigenerational teams. Regardless of the generation to which an individual is born, each generation seems to think the succeeding generation is lacking in some fundamental characteristic that its generation had in abundance. Each generation is quick to cite the differences among the generations and how those differences have a negative impact on the team. Negatives are easy to find and, in many instances, can easily be created.

When establishing communications within multigenerational teams, you should concentrate on similarities within team members. Similarities are much easier to find than you may think, and they can be used to bridge the generational gap.

Take the time to identify each individual's talents and to learn how those talents help the team as well as each individual. Members of all generations can identify quickly and easily with such a list as it provides them with a list of resources for information they may need.

Building a Winning Team

Everyone wants to be on a winning team—it is human nature. People want to be needed; whether it is a sports team or a project team, people have a deep urge to be needed. The question then is how do we turn that urge into a winning team? The answer will surprise you, and I promise to answer that question shortly. First, let's lay out the groundwork.

Building a team is much like building a house—both need a solid foundation and a strong framework. If either of these elements is missing, the team will collapse just as the house would. It is therefore important that, as the team leader, you first establish a solid foundation for your team.

Once the foundation is set, you will then need to work continually on the structure of the team—re-enforcing it as needed, repairing weak areas, and constantly honing the framework of the team until it can stand on its own. Just as a home's frame must endure the forces of nature during a storm to protect its occupants, your team's framework must be solid enough to endure the dynamics of today's business world. Moving deadlines, changing priorities, and flexible budgets are some of the storms your team must endure.

Without a solid foundation and steadfast framework, your team will topple under the constant attack from outside forces. Outside forces such as personal insecurities, the office rumor mill, low morale, low self-esteem, and any number of things will attack your team.

This is all great, right? But how do you do this with your team? Well, as promised, here is your answer. It may surprise you, but successful managers and leaders have used this secret for countless years. Most exceptional managers do not even know they are doing it, but if you ask their teams, you will find evidence of it.

Are you ready? You must make yourself replaceable. Yes, you heard me correctly; I will pause here for a moment while you read that last sentence again.

As I stated in the first chapter, in Building Staff Capacity, to be a good leader, you need to build staff capacity, and to do this, you must build the capacity within your team to handle whatever is sent their way. This is done through delegation, training, and sharing of knowledge.

Let me put it another way. Don't you want to earn more money, move up the corporate ladder, and maybe find yourself on the board of directors or even the chairperson of the board some day? Okay, maybe we are getting a little ahead of ourselves here, but the truth is, there is no reason you cannot move on to the next level of your career. You can achieve anything you set your mind to.

Let's assume for a moment that your company has the perfect job opening available—a job for which you are the perfect candidate, and the salary is incredible! The new position will allow you to achieve your dreams, and best of all, you are ready for it. You have worked hard; you have earned it!

Now imagine sitting in your office when the boss walks in to offer you the position of a lifetime. He looks at you and says, "The job is yours if you can find someone that can replace you in your current position by the end of the day. Your replacement has to know everything you know!"

Could you do that if you were asked? Have you groomed a replacement for your position? Can your team handle things if you suddenly received a promotion? If you want to make yourself so valuable to the organization, you need to be able to answer "yes" to these questions and make yourself replaceable.

Common Ground

The keys to any leader's ability to address critical issues effectively in any organization are the processes used to bring team members together, to deliberate the issues, and to make decisions. In short, as a team leader, it is your job to identify the common ground of all issues. These include project-related issues as well as team issues. It is like building a house—the common ground is where you will lay the foundation on which the home will be constructed. The same is true for your team and the projects on which they work. In order to have a solid foundation for your team, you must find common ground. The logical question is *why*. *What* do you mean by common ground? These are both excellent questions. Let's look at them individually.

To answer *why* you need to find common ground is not always obvious to many managers. The truth is you do not have to find the common ground for your team. Your team is capable of doing it themselves, but it may not be what you want. In home construction, if the ground is too soft, the home will not be stable, and once the foundation has been set, it will be difficult to change it.

Now that we have answered the *why*, let's look at the *what*. As stated earlier, common ground lays the foundation for your team. This binding force will keep them together as a productive unit. It is difficult to determine what the common ground will be for any team, but it is important to choose the common ground quickly.

To decide on your team's common ground, you will need to observe them, watch how they interact with one another, and what motivates them. I cannot tell you what your team's common ground will be. Only you can determine that. Common ground can be nearly anything from practical jokes and laser tag weekends, to team mottos, mission statements, community events or causes, or team Web sites where the team maintains a blog for their interests and interacts with the community through that Web site. A more common example is a team pet project that will benefit from each team member's expertise.

A great example of the use of common ground is the case of Larry and Sergey. Larry and Sergey were not fond of each other when they first met. No matter what the topic of discussion was, they argued about it, in some cases, just for the sake of arguing. They both had strong opinions on nearly every subject.

After some time, the two discovered their common ground. They quickly found that, as different as they were in opinion on most subjects, their differences in viewpoints were essential to the development of software to solve the problem they both had in common—searching for usable data in large databases. Larry and Sergey eventually created one of, if not the, most powerful search engines ever created. Today, millions know their combined talents as Google.com. Larry and Sergey found their common ground, which, as it turned out, was the best choice for them. They could have easily parted ways and simply agreed to disagree with each other.

The right common ground can be the most incredible experience for you and your team. The important thing to remember is to make the choice yourself and then guide your team toward that common ground.

As I stated earlier, if you do not choose a common ground, your team will. The problem with letting the team decide is that the common ground may be negative and non-productive. In cases such as this, the most frequently selected common ground is discussing the boss' inability to lead the team, his thirst for control, his need to crush individuality, or all of the above.

So sit back, examine your team, and choose wisely what the common ground will be. After all, it must support the foundation of your team, which will in turn support the framework for all your projects to come.

Communications

George Bernard Shaw won the Nobel Prize in Literature in 1925 and once stated, "The single biggest problem in communication is the illusion that it has taken place." He is uniquely qualified to comment on this subject, as he was a great communicator through his literary works. He, like most authors, understood the importance of communication and the ease with which someone can completely misunderstand a statement if it is not carefully worded.

One of the greatest problems perpetrated by many managers, as well as management in general, is the illusion that they have somehow communicated their requirements for a project when in fact they have only briefly discussed it.

They tend to assume the team somehow knows what is to be done.

This lack of communications has been the downfall of many managers, departments, and even entire companies, simply because of the lack of good communications. Take a moment and think back to all the times you have been in a situation where you have been accused of not performing a task or did the task incorrectly because your supervisor failed to communicate the requirements to you properly.

I have seen programmers spend countless hours developing a report that could have been completed in a matter of minutes had the requirements for the report been properly communicated.

Many people also confuse communication with speaking to one another, but communications goes well beyond spoken words. Many factors play an integral part of communications as well, such as who is making the request, the tone of the request, and the body language. Is the request written or verbal, in person, over the phone, or via e-mail? All these factors are included in communications. It is not just *what* is said, but *how* it is said.

Take the example of the programmer spending hours working on a report that should have only taken minutes. The programmer over engineered the report because the person making the request for the report was the president of the company and did not follow the defined channels of communications. The programmer took the request from the company president as a direct order and a high priority. He also wanted the report to be perfect for the president so that he could make a good impression by producing a report that looked great as well.

By the time the programmer completed the report, the president had grown frustrated and was able to obtain the information the report would have provided from another source. As a result, the president had a perception that the programmer was inept; the programmer perceived a president that has no clue as to what he wants. Valuable programmer time was wasted on a useless report, and the credibility of the information systems department had been seriously damaged.

This type of scenario happens all too often in corporations all over the world, simply because no one communicated properly or through the proper channels. This demoralizes the team members and sets them up for future failures because each time there is miscommunication, the team gets a bad rap for being incompetent. The executive staff in turn views the department as chaotic, poorly managed, and staffed with expensive employees that cannot perform the simplest tasks.

Effective communication is essential to the success of any organization. Without clear communications, team members will begin to develop a project mentally as it is being explained. They will begin with filling information gaps by making assumptions based on past projects and how the new project will interact with previous projects.

To break this cycle, communication channels must be clearly established, explained to all other departments, and most importantly, they must be followed. A breakdown in any of the established communications channels or methods will doom a project to failure.

Your responsibility as the team leader is to formulate the projects and accurately communicate the requirements to your team. Sydney J. Harris summed it up best when he said, "The two words 'Information' and 'Communication' are often used interchangeably, but they signify quite different things. Information is giving out, while communication is getting through."

Respect

Respect is an incredibly powerful force that can motivate people to perform at their very best, whereas lack of respect can equally motivate someone to perform at his very worst. It is important to show respect for your team. Many people are under the impression that respect can only be earned, that it cannot be freely shown to someone that has not earned the respect. To some level, this is true, but respect is an interesting thing. Granted, you cannot demand respect, but respect can be freely given at will.

Confused? Many people are confused when it comes to respect. They wrongly think, "How can I show respect to someone who has not earned my respect," and this would be a fair question. However, the answer is easier than you may think.

Respect is the act of acknowledging the feelings and interests of another party in a relationship. This can be as simple as saying, "Good morning, have a great day," giving him a pay raise, or by hosting an event in his honor.

Respect is very much like a dimmer switch on a lamp; there are many levels of respect, and they vary based on personal relationships. When you meet someone for the first time, the *dimmer switch of respect* is at its lowest setting. As the two people interact and learn about each other, the level will rise. Major advancements in the relationship that are reinforced by trust cause the level to continue to increase, while setbacks in trust as a result of lying, betrayal, or lack of attention cause the level to drop.

Do not confuse position within the organization with respect. Many people have climbed the ladder of success with a total disregard for respect. To paraphrase an old adage, "Show respect for those you pass on the ladder of success, as they are the same people you will pass on your way back down." Showing respect for your fellow team members is a simple thing to do and should be done at every opportunity. Ready for the hard part?

Earning your team's respect! Do not think for a minute that your team is going to respect you simply because you are the boss, the team leader, the manager, or any number of titles the company has bestowed upon you. One of Aesop's fables states, "Fools take to themselves the respect that is given to their office." In other words, do not confuse the respect for your office as respect for you. You may be "The Boss," but you still have to earn your team's respect.

Build Trust

What is trust? Do you really understand what trust is and how it works? I am sure you are saying, "Sure, I know what trust is," and then you would tell me that trust is the mutual shared belief that two people can depend on each other to achieve a common purpose. More comprehensively, trust, as defined by the Merriam-Webster Dictionary, is

> *The willingness of a party (trustor) to be vulnerable to the actions of another party (trustee) based on the expectation that the trustee will perform an action important to the*

trustor, regardless of the trustor's ability to monitor or control the trustee.

Building relationships requires the building of trust. Trust is the expectancy of people that they can rely on your word. It is built through integrity and consistency in relationships. Every team must have trust. Just as firefighters must trust each other with their lives by protecting each other from the dangers of fighting fires so that each firefighter can perform his job efficiently, a well-formed team must have trust in each other as well as the team leader.

Stephen Covey uses something called an emotional bank account in his book *The 7 Habits of Highly Effective People* to assess the trust level you have with someone. Here is how it works. Treat each interaction with someone as a banking transaction. Credit your account each time you have a positive exchange with the person with whom the account has been established, or debit the account each time there is a problem with the relationship.

Like money in a regular bank account, each positive experience adds interest to the emotional bank account. Through regular deposits and interest building, the emotional bank account will grow—but watch out. It is very easy to overdraw that emotional bank account with a single transaction that could put you into emotional bankruptcy with that person.

Naturally, the question at this point is how do you build trust? Listen, understand, and communicate. You cannot establish trust if you cannot listen. A conversation is a relationship. Both speaker and listener play a part, each influencing the other. Instead of being a passive recipient, the listener has as much to do in shaping the conversation as the speaker by listening and making sure he understands what the speaker is saying. This is communication at its best, and you will be amazed as to how fast trust builds, simply by listening and understanding.

Additionally, you cannot build trust if you do not give credit where credit is due. Each time someone achieves a goal or assists in a project, his contribution must not only be acknowledged, but also announced. To do any less, hacks away at any established trust, and eventually, you will reach emotional bankruptcy with your team. They will begin to feel that you are taking credit for their actions.

Trust can take a long time to establish, but one single act of selfishness or perceived violation of that trust can destroy everything you have created with your team, and it will take twice as long to reestablish that trust if it is even possible.

In short, trust is an ingredient—an ingredient most managers overlook in today's busy world. Just as the eggs in a cake bind all the other ingredients together, trust is the basis of all relationships, business or personal.

Accountability

According to legend, when the Romans built an arch, the engineer took such pride in his design that he would stand underneath the arch as the keystone was set in place and the wooden supports removed. In this manner, the engineer assumed complete responsibility for his design. If the arch failed, he also assumed complete accountability for the design.

Today many managers confuse accountability with "blameability" and tend to be more concerned with who did what, and "how will this affect me?" They will quickly look for someone to blame for errors or oversights. In effect, they are looking for volunteers to stand under the arch, as the keystone is set.

Accountability is not something that a manager can assign to an employee or anyone else for that matter. Accountability has to be taken, just like the Roman engineer standing under the arch he designed as the keystone is set in place and the supports removed. The responsibility for performing the task of setting the keystone is in the hands of the builders. If the arch fails, the builders are not accountable; the flattened engineer will have assumed accountability for his design.

In today's world of high tech, if a technologist wipes out a database that he is responsible for, walks into his manager's office, and tells his manager what he did, then that is accountability. He is making himself accountable for his actions.

How many times have you heard a manager quickly blurt out, "Who did it?", "What did you do?", or "Why didn't you do this or that?" when something went wrong or when a deal fell through. If you have heard these questions before, then you know what it is like to deal with a manager with a "Whose fault is it?" attitude. These managers use "blame-ability" to force accountability in an effort to protect their own position.

If you are one of those managers who have made this mistake, take a deep breath, relax, and take comfort in knowing that you are aware of your actions and assume accountability for your actions. Playing the blame game is a sure fire way to get your team to lose respect and trust in you as a leader. It quickly becomes a self-fulfilling prophecy. The manager blames a subordinate, the subordinate loses respect for the manager, the manager feels the tension, and the process continues.

As a leader, it is your responsibility to harvest an environment where your team is willing to assume accountability. Treat your team with dignity and respect, develop a reputation of level thinking, treat everyone fairly, and above all, be accountable to your supervisors, the team, and yourself. Once you do, you will quickly see the roots of accountability take place in your team.

Cohesiveness

In order to have a successful team that can last the test of time and will stick together under extreme pressure, you need to understand team cohesion.

Team types

There are three types of teams in the workplace: formal, ad hoc, and informal.

Formal teams generally describe corporate hierarchy starting at the top of the chain of command on down through the various corporate officers and managers. These formal teams generally stick to formal methods of communication and use sets of rules, procedures, and methods to exchange information and communicate.

The second type of team, usually formed as a project team and tasked with a specific purpose, is known as an ad hoc team. This team uses the specific task to bring the team together by establishing a common goal.

The third team is the informal team. Nearly everyone is a member of an informal team in some manner unless he is a recluse that lives in the mountains, shuns technology, and refuses to interact with anyone, including a pet. Informal teams, simply put, are your friends, family, colleagues, mentors, and anyone else you look to for support—emotionally or professionally.

If you wish to build strong teams, then each of your teams must include the best elements of the other types of teams. Regardless of the type of team you are building, team members need to be able to rely on each other, be able to turn to one another for support, and have clear communications.

I am often asked if there is an optimal size for a team. Can a team be too big or too small? There are no rules that determine the size of a team, except that the larger the team, the more formal it becomes. A corporation with one thousand employees is in fact a team of one thousand. Because of such a large team, communications quickly suffer, personal interaction becomes rare, and emotional and professional support suffers.

When most people discuss the optimal team size, they are usually talking about smaller project teams, or ad hoc teams. My recommendation is to keep the number of team members odd. I know what you are thinking—not odd people, but an odd number of people.

Another important aspect of a successful team is its structure. The most efficient teams generally support close contact among their members. This means keeping your team members as physically close as possible. I have found that team members that are at remote offices, or for some other reason are not at the same physical location as the rest of the team, are not well informed and miss out on most of the team interaction.

Sometimes it is not possible to have all team members nearby. In these situations, it is important to keep team members notified of all information, using the remote member's favorite form of communication. In today's connected world, technologies such as Instant Messaging, video conferencing, and collaborative project Web sites such as wikis, (a collection of web pages designed to enable anyone who accesses it to contribute or modify content using a simplified markup language) are easily accessible and provide a tremendous benefit to remote team members. Team cohesion is often achieved not by the project itself or the common goal the team members share, but by the camaraderie the team members share, the "inside jokes," and other personal interactions that can only be achieved by close personal contact.

It is vital for a successful team that its members experience workflows that bring them together often and allow them to form a structure for decision making on their own. You cannot force the team to have common bonds or shared interests. Forcing common bonds will result in resistance to those bonds and make the team weaker as a group.

Often teams are sent to all day team-building sessions to learn to trust and interact with each other. In my experience, you cannot force team members to trust each other. Either they do or they do not. If they do not trust each other, then it is time to consider exchanging or removing team members.

Do not get me wrong, team-building exercises can be a valuable tool, can bring team members closer together, and can result in a much better team. What I am saying is that team members must begin with a basic trust of their fellow team members so that those bonds can be strengthened, thereby building a stronger team.

Without the basis of trust, you will be wasting your time and energy simply building trust among individual team members, rather than concentrating on building a strong team with strong bonds. Even if the team fails at various tasks within the project, they experience those setbacks together as a team. This helps build team cohesion in a way that cannot be achieved by any other method. In this manner, setbacks become valuable team-building experiences.

Empowering the Team

When talking about team empowerment, most people confuse empowerment with growth. True empowerment is actually a direct function of a working team environment that respects contributions from levels within the team. Empowerment is real and is achievable, but it does not just happen, and it cannot simply be enacted by managerial decree. Responsibility for empowering the team falls directly on the abilities of management to lead.

The operational demands and pressures of their positions weigh most managers down today. The pressure to meet deliverables, create strategy, and concentrate on key performance indicators prevents today's managers and team leaders from concentrating on team empowerment.

Establishing true team empowerment will require a radical change in the working environment. Management must create an environment that supports constructive freedom, which rewards productive trial as well as failure. Yes, failure must be rewarded as well. If your team is afraid to fail, then they will never take the risks that are necessary to expand understanding. Even failure, if properly examined, can provide meaningful and useful information.

Empowering the team will require a change of context as to how management interacts with teams. The traditional top-down hierarchy of business must give way to a more radical partnership with its team members.

One method that has proven valuable is quarterly management reviews. You may be saying that you currently perform management reviews. You may claim that management reviews each team member's workload and contribution on a regular basis. However, your context of the management review would be incorrect.

When I speak of management reviews, I mean team members review management. Every quarter, each manager should present his direct reports with a worksheet on which the team members provide narrative feedback on how their manager or team leader is performing as a leader. Managers would then meet with team members as a group who would then present their feedback directly to the manager. Talks would then ensue regarding the good, bad, and in-between issues. This exercise can be very difficult as most managers and team members are accustomed to the old hierarchical methods of the past.

In environments that have established management reviews, team members have been able to shape the evolution of their working environments by establishing better communication between themselves and management.

Team members become able to hold managers accountable for improvements. If a manager agrees upon a specific deliverable, this method allows the team members to understand that they can hold their manager accountable for their delivery.

Once the team members begin to hold managers accountable, the context of the working environment will have shifted, and empowerment gets a firm foothold. Team members will begin to harness their capabilities to challenge their managers constructively and other team members as well as the company with their own ideas and concepts. Areas of responsibility will broaden, knowledge will expand, new ideas will form, and morale will show significant improvements.

Once true empowerment has taken place, employees at all levels within the team and/or the company will have the influence to change, improve, and grow the organization. They will have been freed of the fear of making mistakes.

Business Context

Most employees go about their duties with blinders on. They perform the same tasks repeatedly without any concept of how their job fits into the "Big Picture." Most managers simply assume everyone knows how it all fits together. In fact, the manager himself may not have a complete understanding of the big picture, but only the portion for which he is responsible.

From the receptionist to the accounts payable clerks, the software programmers to the sales department, everyone should have a complete understanding of how his job fits into the big picture. Sure the accounts payable people understand what they do, and the information systems department understands the technology side of the company, but do all the employees understand how their job effects everyone else's job?

I recently found myself walking into a company that had a great working environment. The employees all boasted of how wonderful the company was and how happy they were to be working there. I was told the company's turnover rate was very low as well.

The first thing I noticed as I entered the offices was the nameplate on the receptionist's desk. Rather than showing her title as "Receptionist," she was the "Director of First Impression." This made me stop and think, "Here is a company that understands the role of the receptionist." Rather than being, "The Receptionist," this person had an important job to do—to make sure the customers' first experience with the company is pleasant and that they are greeted in a positive manner.

As I toured the offices, I noticed more nameplates: accounts payable clerks were "Vendor Relation Specialists," the payroll and benefits department was known as the "Employee Appreciation Department" staffed by "Employee Appreciation Specialists," and the software programmers were known as "Solutions Engineers."

What could all this mean? I thought about it for days. I was impressed with the employee attitudes and the manner in which the company treated its employees. It was clear that every employee understood not only his job but also how it affected the big picture. They understood the business context of not only their jobs but also everyone's job.

The "Director of First Impression" understood that making a customer feel welcomed would make that customer's dealings with the company much more pleasant. The "Employee Appreciation Specialists" understood that it was their job to process the payroll but that the employees wanted to feel needed and appreciated as well.

These employees were not coming to work everyday to perform their jobs; they were coming to work mutually toward a common goal and do everything possible to support their team in achieving that goal, which was the company's mission statement, "To provide excellent products and customer service and enjoy doing it." Even the company's mission statement included a commitment to the employees to ensure they enjoyed providing excellent products and customer service.

I was impressed to say the least. I jotted down page after page of notes on how to implement these incredible methods into any organization. I even asked for a job application for myself. I was informed they do not hand out job applications. They call them "Team Membership Applications."

I walked away thinking about the possibilities of having such a dream job, when a loud buzzing sound startled me. It seemed to come from everywhere. Just then I reached out, pressed the snooze button, and tried desperately to slip back to sleep to experience just a few more minutes of my dream job before I too must wake up and go to work.

Yes, this was a dream, but it was based in reality. The titles are real, I have seen them used in many organizations, and they do have a positive psychological effect on the employee's attitudes.

Many businesses are slowly implementing many of these methods, as they become aware of the importance of making sure the employees understand the business context of their jobs and can see the big picture.

DaVita is a prime example of this concept in action. DaVita Inc. is the largest provider of dialysis services in the United States for patients suffering from chronic kidney failure. DaVita does not consider itself and its employees in the traditional sense; rather, they view the employees as citizens of the corporate village.

DaVita takes the education of its citizens very seriously and has taken the idea of business context to its extreme with the formation of the DaVita Academy where employees are educated in the history of the village and how the village works. The Academy does not teach them how to be more productive or how to do their jobs; it concentrates on the employees' wellbeing and integration into the village and insuring that each citizen understands the business context and the mission of the village.

Teams vs. Groups

A working group's performance is a function of what its members do as individuals. You take the work, divide it into person-hours, and portion it off. The metric for how well a working group member performs is how well they complete the person-hours of work apportioned them.

Since individual accountability is a convenient thing to have, most organizations use working groups. Most committees, councils, task forces, and "teams" are really working groups. These groups are usually called "teams," since team sounds good, but saying something is a team does not automatically make it one.

Working groups generally have the following characteristics:

- A strong leader that micromanages
- Individual accountability, fostering attitude of self-preservation
- Organizational purpose

- Individual work products
- Efficient meetings to assign work
- Performance measured by influence on others
- Delegated work
- Focus on accountability of individual tasks

Working groups are not inferior to teams! Sometimes they are the quickest, most effective way to get the job done on a small scale.

Now, teams, on the other hand, require both individual and mutual accountability. They rely on more than group discussion, debate, and decision. They rely on sharing information and best-practice performance standards. They produce work through the joint contributions of their members. They make possible performance levels that are greater than the individuals of the team are capable of on their own.

Teams demonstrate the following characteristics:

- Shared leadership
- Individual & mutual accountability
- Specific team purpose
- Collective work products
- Open-ended meetings
- Performance measured for work products

- Real work done together

Members are motivated by clear, mutual goals. Their performance includes both individual results and collective work products. However, teams go further by enabling one individual's thought process to merge with another's. Employees thrive on the interaction that only a true team can provide.

Take a symphony, for example. Each member must work in harmony with each other to create music that is enjoyable to the audience. However, if each member of the symphony were to play his part of the musical score at his own pace and without regard for the other members of the symphony, you would still have the same musical score, but no one would want to listen to the noise.

A team is the same as the symphony. They each know their individual instruments. For your employees, it may be computers, calculators, and payroll and accounting systems. But unless each team member understands the common goal, what you will end up with is a group of individuals marching to the beat of a different drummer. Your job as team leader is like that of the conductor, keeping everyone in harmony.

Teams do not have to be working on the same project, whereas working groups congregate around a job at hand and dissolve when the job is finished. Teams endure past the completion of an assignment.

Teams remember past projects and how those projects will interact with each of the components of the new project. Groups, on the other hand, have to be trained or brought up to speed each time a new project is created since no individual members may be familiar with any other component of the previous projects.

The most effective leaders never say "I." It is not that they avoid saying "I"; they think in terms of "we." They think of the team, and they understand that their job is to create a better team through effective coaching. They accept their responsibility and do not try to take credit for the team. Instead, they give the team credit for all successes. The outstanding leader, however, takes sole responsibility for the team's failures. This creates trust, builds character, and drives an excellent team.

Building Confidence

Confidence is one of the most important characteristics of any leader. Whether you are in sales, marketing, accounting, or information systems, you will radiate confidence or, in some cases, lack of it.

Confidence is very much like a lighthouse, shining bright and guiding ships around dangerous waters. When you have confidence in the company, the project, and your team, you shine like that lighthouse, reassuring everyone that you are there to guide them through the troubles that may threaten a project.

At the simplest level, you must have confidence in your team. Without it, your team will feel disconnected and mistrusted, causing stress to build, and your team will begin to second-guess the project, their tasks, and themselves. Confidence in your team is one of the strongest motivators you have to keep your team productive. If you have confidence in your team's abilities and confidence in the project, you will naturally radiate that confidence, your team will feel it and be stronger because of it, and they too will have confidence in you as a leader. Your confidence will reassure them that what they are doing is valuable to the team, the project, and the company.

Confidence in your team and their abilities also shows them that you respect them as individuals. Your team will respond in kind and have confidence in your abilities to lead, in some cases, blindly, confident that you have a clear vision of the big picture.

Chinese philosopher Lao-Tse once said, "A leader is best when people barely know he exists. Not so good when people obey and acclaim him, worse when they despise him. 'Fail to honor people, they fail to honor you.' But of a good leader, who talks little, when his work is done, his aim fulfilled, they will say, 'he is a great leader!'"

Lao-Tse understood that having confidence in your team and trusting them to get things done is what makes a great leader. Micromanaging, watching over your team, and nit picking every action does not show confidence in your team, quickly demoralizes the team members, and builds a barrier—sometimes an impenetrable barrier. It is best to simply back off, and let your team do what they are good at.

This reminds me of a great story that I read in the book *Catch Me if You Can* by Frank Abagnale, Jr. Frank was a check forger and imposter for five years in the 1960s. During his five-year crime spree, he worked under no fewer than eight identities, one of which was as a pediatrician named Frank Connors in a Georgia hospital.

Frank chose to retire in Georgia after he discovered the FBI was closing in on him. He created his character Frank Connors as a pediatrician from out-of-state, figuring he would never be asked any real medical questions or be called to practice medicine. Unfortunately, he befriended a neighbor that turned out to be a doctor at a local hospital.

One day, his friend called him with a problem. He explained to Frank that he was in a jam. He needed a doctor to cover the night shift at the hospital. Frank objected and explained that he was not licensed to practice medicine in Georgia. His friend assured him he would not have to. He explained that the hospital had several interns, and he simply had to keep an eye on them. Frank was then reassured that nothing ever happens on the night shift, and it was only for a short period, maybe a week.

Well, weeks became months, and Frank had figured out that the interns could handle just about anything that happened. When the interns had an issue and did not know what to do, Frank showed confidence in their abilities by asking the interns what they felt should be done with a patient. Once the answer was given, Frank would then ask a second intern if he concurred with the first intern. If he did, Frank would simply tell them "good work, looks like you know what you are doing" and would walk away.

Do not get me wrong. I am not condoning what Frank did by any means whatsoever. In fact, Frank finally quit when he realized his actions could cost someone his life. Frank notified his friend that he would no longer be able to continue, and fortunately, a replacement was located.

The interesting thing about this story, however, is not Frank or his crimes, or that he was the ultimate confidence man. The interesting part was what the interns said about "Dr. Frank Connors" after he left. Unaware that Frank Connors was a fraud, they claimed he was the best doctor with whom they had ever had the honor of working. They said they learned more about medicine under Frank than from any other doctor to date.

I know what you are thinking, and I thought the same thing. Let me explain. The interns claimed that all the other doctors would always jump in and take charge. The interns would be pushed aside and simply watch the doctors perform their work. Frank, on the other hand, let them do what they were trained to do in medical school—practice medicine.

The point is that confidence is a powerful motivator, which can make your team perform miracles if you let them. Show you have confidence in your team by backing off and letting them do what they have been trained to do, and some day, they may make the same statements about your great leadership.

Delegate

When it comes to guiding your team, getting the project completed within the allotted time and within budget are the primary objectives. To do this, you must learn to delegate. You have taken the time to assemble an excellent team. You have worked long and hard to build their trust, and you have learned to trust them. It is now time to start dividing the workload.

Too many managers feel that they are losing control by delegating. If you are a manager, then learn to delegate, hand that control to your team, and trust them to get the job done. If you do not learn to delegate, your projects will be late, over budget, and you will look incompetent.

Bruce Barton, an American author, advertising executive, congressman in the United States House of Representatives from 1937 to 1941, and one of the greatest advertising minds ever once said, "You can get a lot more done if you're not concerned about who gets the credit for it."

Take the time to delegate assignments to your team and give them enough room to get the tasks done on their own. In other words, once you have assigned a task, do not hang out over them, pushing to get the task done. If you do stand over them, they will feel you do not trust them, they will be nervous, they will most likely make mistakes, and as a result, the task will take longer than it should.

I have seen many managers make the mistake of assigning a task to a team member only to become frustrated that it is taking longer than they would like. Out of frustration, the manager will complete the task on his own. When the team member finally completes the task, he discovers his manager has already completed the task. This can be a crushing blow to the team member's confidence.

If you do not feel a task is progressing fast enough, do not take it upon yourself to complete it and leave your team members simply going through the motions. Talk to the person it was assigned to, discuss your concerns, and try to discover why the task is taking so long. There could be many issues as to the cause of the delay—reasons you may not have foreseen yourself.

When planning your team's work assignments, do not fall into the ego trap. Far too many managers assign the monotonous tasks they do not want to perform to their team while keeping the high profile tasks for themselves. Delegation is not about assigning tasks that you do not want; it is about getting the most quality work done as possible within the shortest period while using the resources available to their fullest.

Yes, this means that even those ideal tasks you would love to do yourself should be delegated to your team. In fact, as the team leader, you have a responsibility to keep your team motivated, and sometimes, this might mean that you may have to take on your share of the problem tasks.

Ronald Reagan said, "Surround yourself with the best people you can find, delegate authority, and don't interfere as long as the policy you've decided upon is being carried out."

Leading the Team

We live in a world that faces unseen changes. Within organizations, we see managers struggling to come to terms with new demands on their managerial and leadership style. We have shifted from a position where control is managed by virtue of a formal badge of office (manager, parent, director, etc.) to one where we have to lead people using more intangible and flexible forms of leadership. Employees no longer accept the "do what I say" regime. They respond to a "do what I do" leadership style.

If you are to lead others more effectively, you have to get serious about the idea of personal leadership rather than the old-fashioned leadership of decades past. This is leadership where the whole you is aligned, centered, and able to build relationships with anyone with whom you work. You must expand your personal leadership potential by working from the inside out, understanding how you map and manage the world and ultimately what action you can take to achieve your goals.

Know where you are going first. There is little point in leading technologists unless you know where you are taking them. The goal is to define a set of clear personal goals and outcomes and to use these as criteria by which future choices are taken. If you do not know where it is you are going, then any decision you make today will likely be sub-optimal and will often need to be taken repeatedly. This leads you and your team to follow other people's goals, which are also sub-optimal.

At the end of the day, any leadership action will generally result in some form of change. Consequently, it is imperative to understand what change leadership style is adopted and how effective it is. If you do what you always did, you will get what you always got. For any transition to be effective and sustainable, you will need to learn how to affect change using alternative styles.

To deliver personal success that is sustainable effectively, you need to understand what success is for your technologists. To do this, it is important to step outside of your view of the world and into theirs. Only once you understand how others think, feel, and behave, can you truly understand what success looks like for them.

Leadership that is selfish and short-lived is not true leadership. The only real form of personal leadership is one that is founded in the notion of shared outcomes and sustainable success.

Leader vs. Manager

There have been countless books on the subjects of leadership and just as many on management. Many times the terms *leader* or *manager* are used interchangeably, but they are two very separate entities and are rarely found in the same individual.

A manager is a hierarchy term used to describe a person's position within an organization. This person generally controls or directs workers by making plans that advance the organization's goals and objectives. An organizational hierarchy is by definition a control structure, so as you can see, to manage a team is to control a team.

Teams do not respond well to control. In fact, control is the last thing you want when it comes to creating a productive team. Even the term *team* is in conflict with the term *manager.* A team is a distinguishable set of two or more individuals who interact dynamically, interdependently, and adaptively to achieve a specified set of objectives. A team is not a control structure, but a collaborative structure based on the sharing of ideas and concepts.

A leader, on the other hand, is someone that *shows the way* and requires visibility, credibility, and integrity to perform his job and lead a team to their goals and objectives. A leader must create rapport with his team and is, in fact, a member of the team, unlike a manager who simply hands down directives to the team, usually through its leader.

A leader is someone who understands what the driving forces are for an individual and can exploit them for the benefit of the team in meeting their objectives. In addition to understanding the individual team members, a good leader clears the road ahead of the team, allowing them to perform to their best abilities.

In stark contrast, a manager is someone who understands what needs to be delivered, by when, and at what cost. Managers are focused on key performance indicators and are concerned with measurements and reports.

Rarely are the qualities of a good manager and a good leader found in the same person, yet we often expect it. The art is learning to combine these two contrasting talents by using Your Guiding Genius.

Foster Inclusion

Everyone wants to fit in. They want to be a part of something bigger than themselves. They want to make a difference and to be recognized for their contributions—not because of selfishness or vanity, but to leave their mark on something that will hopefully live long after they are gone.

In order to motivate your team, you will need to create an inclusive team. Bringing together the various talents and viewpoints that a diverse team possesses will result in a team that has the abilities to tackle complex problems.

It is important to understand that inclusion extends beyond ethnicity and gender to include diversity of attitudes, values, and ways of thinking. You will need to give your team members the space to grow, to be themselves, to exercise their diversity. You need to give your team members space so that they may both give and receive such things as ideas, openness, dignity, joy, healing, and inclusion.

This is perhaps one of the most compelling arguments for teamwork. In a team-based environment, each member will bring knowledge and perspectives that will allow other team members to view issues in a way they never would on their own, thereby enhancing the team's abilities and insights.

Once you have established an inclusive work environment for your team, you will be amazed at how quickly the benefits are realized. Benefits such as improved communication, cooperation, and mentoring are just a few.

Your team members will begin to seek out advice of other team members instinctively without fear of having their ideas stolen or circumvented. Because all team members are included in problem solving, decision making, and all other areas of importance, they will be more apt to share their perspective on issues.

I am not saying that your team needs to be included in every single meeting, decision, or issue that should arise. What I am saying is that if something involves a team member or a project a team member is working on, then that team member should be given the option to be a part of the discussion and should have the opportunity to make his point of view heard.

Sometimes just asking if he would like to sit in on a meeting can make all the difference in how a team member perceives the work environment. One of the quickest ways to build paranoia within a team is to exclude a team member from meetings and decisions that affect his projects.

It takes an exceptional leader to open the channels of communication enough to foster inclusion within his team and feel secure enough to allow the ideas of his team members to be realized.

Define Done

What is *done*? Can something ever be *done*? Anyone that has children can attest to the fact that *done* is a subjective term at best. Some things can never be *done*.

I grew up writing software, and to this day, I will come across a piece of software I may have written years ago. When I look at it, I usually say, “What was I thinking?” I immediately identify the sections that can be optimized—a better structure for this and a better formula for that. So I will go about changing the program, cleaning it up, making it better than before. Years later, I will then look at that exact same program, think the exact same phrase as before, and then proceed to clean up the program some more.

The reason I continuously find ways to improve the program is simple. Time has passed. I have expanded my knowledge and my understanding of the world, the business, and the programming language. Therefore, when I view the program, I am looking at it with new insight. As a result, that one program in my mind will never be *done*.

The same holds true for most projects. Your team members may begin the project with a particular mindset and halfway through the project, have some epiphany that causes the whole project to become clear to them. In that "aha!" moment, the team member, or members, may have instantly viewed every problem within the project that has been completed to date. Team members may be drawn back to revisit those completed tasks and improve on them.

Given the opportunity, a project may never be done. There are only levels of doneness. Team members will forever find ways to improve methods, improve systems, or process information.

With each project your team works on, they are gaining knowledge— knowledge that can be used to improve previous projects or sections of the current projects. Therefore, when creating project specifications, it is imperative that you establish what *done* means. The project specifications may need a variety of conditions in order to be placed into production; there may also be many requirements that are not as critical. By defining *done*, it is more likely that you will meet your target date for your projects, and with every completed project, comes a boost to morale.

As for those endless modifications to existing projects that your team will conjure up? Have them create revision notes for those times when work is slow or when the team needs a boost. It will make them feel great to have a list of improvements that can be made to past projects.

Promote Upward Management

Many teams I have interviewed have had a manager at some point that was well respected by their teams but was ineffective when dealing with upper management, while other managers were ineffective because they did not know how to manage office politics to their advantage effectively, to "work the system," so to speak.

On the other hand, you may be a frustrated manager or team member that cannot seem to get your supervisor to do what you need done. Regardless of the situation in which you find yourself, either the manager dealing with upper management or a team member dealing with your own manager, there is hope.

Lonnie Pacelli, an internationally recognized author and president of Leading on the Edge International (projectmanagementadvisor.com), has advised many Fortune 500 companies on upward management, and he explains it this way:

> *Upward management is one of those skills that some do very well, others may never seem to master, and virtually all learn only through on-the-job lessons learned. When done well, both the manager and employee work as a team to ensure that the other is informed. They address problems together before they spin out of control and, as a result,*

are more effective at managing. When done poorly, both manager and employee are not only ineffective at getting the job done but are chronically frustrated due to poor planning and unexpected events.

Poor upward managers can be categorized into four personality types:

The brown-noser. This employee treats his boss as some kind of rock star and constantly searches for what his boss wants to hear. He is only interested in obtaining his boss's approval, and rather than upwardly manage, he upwardly affirms whatever the boss is saying.

The rebellious teenager. This type of employee consciously conceals information from his boss because he wants to demonstrate that he can get things done without help from his boss. Rather than upwardly managing, the rebellious teenager keeps his manager in the dark by withholding information.

The cowardly lion. This employee simply is afraid to share information with his boss because he fears his boss's reactions. Rather than upwardly managing, the cowardly lion avoids sharing information unless he has no alternative but to share the information.

The erupting volcano. This employee subscribes to the "more is better" school of information management, and she will tell her manager every gory detail of every single event every single day. This employee makes it all too obvious as to how difficult a task is and what is involved in painstaking detail. Rather than upwardly managing, the erupting volcano spews data like hot lava and forces the manager to pick out the important facts.

So how do you avoid the pitfalls of managing upward? Consider the following steps and you will be well on your way to managing upward:

Understand your boss. Think about how your boss likes to communicate: Does he prefer written e-mails or verbal discussion? Does he like structured one-on-one meetings or informal chats? Get a clear understanding of how your boss likes to engage, and adapt your style to his style.

Stick to objective facts. When presenting information, avoid emotionally biased assessments. Sure, you may have put your heart and soul into a project, but if the project no longer makes business sense to do, then it is your responsibility to put personal feelings aside and do the right business thing.

Do not dump problems on your manager's doorstep that you should be solving yourself. Yes, your manager has greater responsibility than you have, probably is paid more than you are, and most likely has more organizational influence than you. That does not mean you get to delegate things you should be solving yourself. Handle the problems that you are paid to handle and enlist your manager for the things that require his influence in the organization.

Be specific about what you need. Whether it is money, resources, or some other form of assistance, be very specific about what you need, why you need it, and what will happen if you do not get what you need. Credible objectivity is crucial here: if it looks as if you are stacking the deck by exaggerating consequences or embellishing benefits, you are not likely to get what you need. In addition, subsequent requests are going to be viewed with greater skepticism.

Do not ever give your manager reason to question your credibility. Simply put, if you are caught stretching the truth on even the smallest of facts, you have now given your manager reason to question not only the little things but also the big things. You have to stay pure with your manager and protect your integrity by never allowing your credibility to be put to question.

Do not manage upward at the expense of managing downward. I have known one too many managers who did a great job of keeping their bosses happy but had a team that wanted to string them up by their thumbs.

At some point in time, those that manage up at the expense of managing down will be found out and will have to pay the price. Do not play Russian roulette with your career by keeping your manager comfortable while alienating your team.

Respect your manager's time. If you have a meeting with your boss, show up on time, come prepared to discuss whatever topics need discussing, and end the meeting on time. Your boss is busy and his time should be utilized as effectively as possible. Do not let your manager view your meetings as a waste of time.

Diligently follow through on commitments. Your manager asks you to complete an assignment by tomorrow. You agree to meet the commitment. The deadline passes, you have not met the commitment, and all you can offer up is some lame excuse.

Even if you think an assignment given to you is the dumbest assignment on earth, if you have made a commitment to do it, then meet the commitment. By not following through, you are showing lack of respect for your manager and breeding distrust.

Present options. In decision making, managers like to see alternatives and the consequences associated with each alternative. Some of the best decision-making meetings I have been in with my manager have been where we had meaningful dialogue around two or three viable options in order to resolve a difficult problem.

My job in the process was to frame up the options, provide facts to support each option, and provide a recommendation. Sometimes the recommendation was taken, sometimes not; the most important thing was that a good decision was made because there was good informed discussion.

Make your manager look good. Let's say that your manager is due to make a presentation to his boss and is relying upon you to provide some critical information. You give your manager the information he needs, and he presents it to his boss. He then is reprimanded because the information is wrong. Guess whose office he stops at first on his way back from being barbecued? Simply put, do not put your manager in a situation where he looks bad in front of his management; you have not only hurt your credibility, you have hurt his credibility.

Do not suck up. Telling your manager what he wants to hear will label you as a brown-noser who does not have the fortitude to manage effectively on your own. You will not only quickly lose the respect of your team; your manager will ultimately see through you and not respect your leadership abilities. Sure, you may get the occasional self-absorbed manager that craves shameless idolatry, but largely, managers view sucking up as incompetence.

No surprises. Have you ever told your manager that your project was on schedule and on budget, and then at the last minute you sprung a huge schedule or budget slip on him? Particularly, early in my career, I have had this happen more than once. For it to happen more than once is shameful to say the least. Managers do not like surprises where they are forced to accept a problem without having the option to try to fix it before it got out of control. When you see problems, make sure you notify your manager; then make sure you are working diligently to resolve the problem rather than simply protecting yourself.

Admit mistakes quickly. Mistakes happen. We have all had our fair share of mistakes, usually more that we care to let our managers know about. The important thing is to own up to your mistakes quickly and outline what you are going to do to rectify the mistake. Being the last one to recognize you have made a mistake just diminishes your credibility, so own up to those gaffes and start fixing them.

Upward management: sometimes a real pain, many times a diversion, but always a necessity. Take stock of your upward management skills, and see where you might need to tie up some loose ends, using some, if not all, of these tips.

Those people who have been successful at managing upwardly have established a relationship with their manager in which they are perceived as being credible and trustworthy. In order to accept explicitly or implicitly your attempts at upward management, your manager must view you as being someone who contributes value to discussions and decisions that must be made. Your manager must also see you as someone whom they can trust, based on experiences.

Once the perception of trust has been established, you must demonstrate the ability to provide substantive value to the decision-making process, bringing value to the discussion in the form of insight, ideas, and suggestions. Further, you should have a proven record of accomplishment of success in terms of decision-making ability. You must come to the table prepared to do the hard work to generate alternatives and to do what it takes to support the leader in any given situation without sacrificing morals, values, integrity, and ethics.

Represent the Team

I have seen this repeatedly, and it never ceases to amaze me as to how shallow some managers are in terms of giving credit where credit is due. I am sure everyone has been in this situation before. You work hard on a project and give it 110 percent, and as a result, you may have done your best work ever, only to have your supervisor claim credit for the project as if he did all the work without even mentioning your contribution. If you have, then you know how infuriating it can be.

I have experienced this situation numerous times both as an employee that has had to endure managers such as this and as a director that has had countless managers come to me attempting to take the spotlight for others' hard work.

This behavior by a manager is the most deplorable act any manager can do to his team. This behavior discounts the team's value to management and actually works against the manager. If upper management knows that a team leader or department manager is attempting to claim sole credit for his team's work, he loses the respect of upper management. However, if upper management is unaware of these blotted claims, then management may begin to think the manager does not need a team. The team may be redistributed, leaving the manager to continue his outstanding productivity on his own—and I am sure his team would love to observe the results of that situation.

These self-serving individuals generally have very short careers and are usually very insecure in their positions. They do not understand the value of a team leader's position and are too busy competing with the team they are supposed to be leading in order to manage it effectively. These feelings of insecurity are usually a self-fulfilling prophecy. These types of team leaders get in over their heads and eventually are terminated, reinforcing the feeling of insecurity. Therefore, they are destined to repeat these mistakes repeatedly.

If you are going to be successful as a team leader, you need to represent the team. You are their eyes and ears when dealing with management. Therefore, make sure you represent the team and give credit where credit is due. Make sure awards that you present to team members are broadcast company-wide. An award given in secrecy is not an award.

Just as a famous television and movie star has a manager that promotes the star and builds his image to the public, your job is to build the image of your team to the company. Remember, your team has the skills the company needs to be competitive. You have the skills to make that team the best they can be and promote them just as movie stars' managers do for their clients.

Interacting with Your Team

Interpersonal relationships at work serve a critical role in the development and maintenance of trust in any organization. However, the quality of the relationship alone is not sufficient to maintain the productivity of your team. As the team leader, you must abstain from showing favoritism while making difficult choices that sometimes are not very popular; at the same time, show concern for each of your team members without prying into personal lives, and do all this without misusing the authority of your position.

Often new team leaders are instructed to maintain a healthy distance from workers, which is often difficult for those that have risen through the ranks and have formed personal relationships with those they now manage. Yet as the team leader, you must be approachable and objective, all the while keeping a fair, yet firm, grip on your team. This is often easier said then done.

A good lesson can be learned from the area of sales. Salespersons know that customers enjoy having their egos stroked. Stroking, in this context, refers to verbal or physical acknowledgement of another person's value and is a basic element of human interaction.

Stroking can be a simple pat on the back, a congratulatory handshake, or a verbal comment acknowledging the team member's contribution. If you are a football fan, odds are you have witnessed the members of your favorite team patting each other on the back or rubbing each other's helmets after scoring a touchdown. This is stroking, and it is very common in athletics.

In the sales arena, it is common for a salesperson to compliment a client's knowledge in a particular field or their understanding of an issue in an attempt to make the customer feel comfortable and thereby provide more information that will allow the salesperson to achieve his objectives, such as a signed contract.

I must also note that it is important to know what type of *stroking* your team members will accept. I once read about a case of stroking that did not work as intended. It all started when the daughter of the owner of a company reported that an employee mistook her friendly pats on the back, intended to convey thanks for a job well done, as a romantic interest on her part. It made for an awkward situation. I therefore suggest caution be used when dealing with your team members. What works for one team member may backfire with another.

The Art of Appreciation

It is easy to take your team members for granted. In today's fast-paced world of business, we often overlook how those projects are done. They do not just happen on their own; there are people behind all those little tasks that when combined, become more than the sum of their parts. They become completed projects.

Each one of us has a need to feel appreciated. It is a basic instinct in all people to be needed, to be appreciated, and to be recognized for our achievements. William James, a pioneering psychologist and philosopher, recognized this in the late nineteenth century when he said, "The deepest principle in human nature is the craving to be appreciated."

Employees do not live on salary alone. They need self-esteem. Appreciation is how you can help build self-esteem in your team and in yourself. You will find that by showing appreciation for your employees' work, they will in turn appreciate you and the appreciation you show for them. It is a win-win situation for everyone; why not start showing your appreciation now?

"Appreciation is a wonderful thing: It makes what is excellent in others belong to us as well" (Voltaire).

Many managers are too busy looking at the bottom line to worry about appreciation. They incorrectly think, "Why show appreciation for something that they are supposed to do." They do not understand how appreciation can directly affect the bottom line.

You have a lot of time and money invested in your employees. They have been trained to perform specific job duties, and this took time and money. What would happen if that employee decided to quit? How would that affect your team, your projects, and your bottom line?

Turnover is bad for the bottom line; it disrupts teams and delays projects. If a team member leaves and is replaced, your team must learn how to deal with a new member, the new team member must learn how to deal with the other team members, and you have to learn how your new employee will affect the team and the projects on which they are working.

Even if you do not replace an exiting team member, you still have to deal with redistributing the tasks that team member performed on a daily basis. This requires additional training for the other team members who are expected to pick up the slack.

I came across an interesting story about a woman named Susan that highlights the importance of appreciation. Susan had worked for a large corporation for over thirty years. She never received a bad review and always performed her duties with skill and determination. Susan was committed to the company in every respect. She was rarely sick and always willing to do what was necessary for the company because she felt appreciated.

Susan's supervisor always offered a compliment when she completed a project or went the extra mile to get something done. Susan's supervisor frequently bought her lunch or dropped movie tickets on her desk.

As is common in many businesses today, Susan's boss left the company and started his own business. About a week later, Susan was informed that her job would now be under the supervision of one of the directors of another department. The department was known to have high turnover, but Susan did not feel this would be a problem as her job duties or responsibilities would not change. She figured everything would be the same.

It did not take long for Susan to find out things had changed. As usual, she completed her projects with extreme detail. Then she completed another project and another. She started to miss her old boss. She thought about all the compliments, the movie tickets, and the little thank-you notes.

That is when it hit her. Her job had become a "job." It was no longer enjoyable. She started going home on time like everyone else in the department. She no longer worked overtime or went the extra mile. Susan started taking shortcuts on her projects; she only did what was required for the job.

One day her phone rang. She answered it, and it was her old boss. They talked for a while, and she filled him in on the changes in the company. She described, in detail, how her new boss could not care less about the employees, how productivity was down, and the turnover was high.

In the middle of their conversation, Susan's old boss interrupted and asked her if she would consider working for him at his new company. He explained to her that it would be a pay cut, and the health benefits were not as good, but he explained that with her assistance, he was confident the company would be a success. Rumor has it she was in his office before he could hang up the phone!

Listen and You Will Hear

Can you remember the last conversation you had with one of your team members? Do not feel bad if you cannot remember. The average untrained listener retains only 50 percent of a conversation within the last four hours. After 48 hours, the retention rate drops to less than 25 percent and to almost 10 percent after 96 hours.

To get the most out of your team members, you will need to learn to listen. Really listen to what they have to say, even if it is not what you want to hear or if you think you know exactly what they are going to say.

Attentively listening to your team members tells them, individually and as a group, that they matter—that you think they are important. This goes a long way towards building trust and making the team understand that you are there to help and lead. Therefore, when a team member enters your office to talk, put your work away. It will still be there when you are done talking.

Resist the urge to interrupt and complete their thoughts. As hard as it may be, you should bite your tongue and listen until he has completed explaining his thoughts. If you jump in mid-sentence and interrupt him, he may lose his train of thought, making the conversation much more difficult to understand and follow. It also tells the team members that you are in a hurry and want to get finished as quickly as possible. Even if this is true, resist the temptation to push the conversation along in this manner. In the end, rushing the conversation only makes it take longer and be less productive.

Once he has completed his thought, ask questions, restate what he just said, and make sure you understand what he means. This will tell your team member that you care and truly desire to help him.

This is your chance to listen and learn. If done correctly, this can be the most rewarding part of your job. Just listen, and you may hear something you never knew before. An ancient proverb says, "Incompetent people always think they are right, while wise people listen to advice and learn from it."

Team members may seek a private meeting with you for any number of reasons, ranging from personal issues to complex ideas. If one of your team members comes to you expressing concern over a personal issue, take the time to listen and understand what your team member is telling you. It may be trivial to you, but to her, it may be an important issue.

If a team member comes to you with a personal issue, such as money or family issues, and is expressing a need for help, you owe it to the individual, as well as the team, to help if possible. The help required may simply be emotional support or understanding while the employee is going through a difficult time.

If you fail to help, then the problem will grow until it consumes most of the individual's time. Production will drop, quality of work will drop, and it will not be long before other team members are affected. Other times, team members may have an idea that they simply want to bounce off you. It may be to improve a current process or to understand an issue better.

Take the time to talk and discuss the issue. Often I have had team members enter my office shortly after a meeting with an idea or question that should have been brought up in the meeting they just completed. Team members will often do this if they lack confidence in their own abilities or are unsure of their own idea. In either case, they fear having their idea rejected by the group attending the meeting.

In cases such as this, listen to them and examine the issue. If the idea is sound, tell them and help them present the idea at the next meeting. Help them build the confidence they need to present the idea to the team. Even if the idea is not very good but can act as a catalyst for other ideas, encourage the team member to present the idea as a starting point.

You have invested a great deal of time and money in each of the team members. They are on your team because they have the knowledge, expertise, and know-how to get the job done. So take the time to listen to the experts you hired for your team. After all, they just might have that next million-dollar idea that will get you and your team promoted.

Compromise

What is compromise? According to the Merriam-Webster dictionary, "compromise is the settlement of differences by arbitration or by consent reached by mutual concessions." This is great if we are talking about a child's game, a personal relationship, or simply cutting a piece of cake to share, but in business, compromise simply does not work.

In business, compromise should be a last resort. If two teams or employees have a difference of agreement as to how an issue should be handled, and they cannot resolve it themselves, then as the manager, it is up to you to listen to both sides and then pick one or the other. By choosing a clear winner, solid responsibility for success will be clearly placed on the winning team or employee to make the idea work.

It should also be noted that upon listening to both sides, there is the possibility that you, as the manager, may not like either idea or resolution the parties are advocating. In situations such as this, compromise may seem to be the logical next step, but in reality, compromise is out of the question. To pick between two poor ideas, or worse, to compromise between two bad ideas, is setting the foundation for failure. Margaret Thatcher once said, "If you just set out to be liked, you would be prepared to compromise on anything at any time, and you would achieve nothing."

It is best to reject both ideas or views and simply tell them why you do not like the ideas, task them to explore other possibilities, and then return with a solution that will work. This is often the only method that will work.

Often the reason the ideas are poor is that the involved parties begin to take it personally. They feel the other party is rejecting their ideas, and they feel that sense of rejection and naturally take hold in defense. This more often clouds the real issues and results in the correct resolution being overlooked. By rejecting both ideas, you level the playing field for both parties and send them both back to the drawing board with a fresh perspective. As a manager, you have a responsibility to the company to ensure that all decisions are for the good of the organization.

Compromise is not a method for building up companies. It is a method for keeping the peace, and peace won by compromise is a short-lived achievement.

It Is Not What You Say; It Is How You Say It

Napoleon Bonaparte once said, "An order that can be misunderstood will be misunderstood." As any parent can attest to, sometimes it is not what you say that causes confusion, but how you say it. Your tone or inflection can easily be misunderstood while making a simple request or offering your answer to a request. This concept becomes even more of an issue when dealing with team members where English is not their first language or those that do not have a proper understanding of sarcasm.

It is therefore important to choose your words carefully when making a request or offering a response. I have witnessed many managers give a positive response in a sarcastic tone indicating a negative response, only to watch in total frustration as an employee that misunderstood the comment proceeded to do exactly what the manager did not want him to do.

When dealing with your team members, take care in not only what you say, but also in how you say it. Be careful of your tone, and make sure you do not belittle any of your team members. As I stated previously, tone and inflection can cause misunderstandings and result in incorrect interpretation of your requests. How you treat others also determines how they will react to your requests and whether your requests will be followed.

If you belittle your team members, they will have very little respect for you. Even if you only belittle one of the team members once, other team members will quickly notice and may think less of you as their manager. No one wants to work for a bully.

Make sure you treat all team members as valuable team members. Show them the respect that they deserve, and you will be rewarded with enthusiastic team members that want to show you how valuable they are to the team. They will show you the respect that you deserve as well.

In addition to making sure you do not belittle your team members, you must also be careful not to belittle the situation. When a team member comes to you with a problem, take the time to listen and listen to understand. You may think the problem is trivial, but to the team member, it may be a big issue.

Let them provide you with the relevant information. If you need more information, ask for it in a respectable manner with the intent to understand the situation. Once you understand, and you have placed yourself in your team member's position, you will be prepared to offer suggestions or a complete solution but do so in a respectable manner.

People and situations are not the only thing that managers routinely belittle. Often, the actions team members take are belittled as well. This form of belittling takes place most often when someone consistently performs well. If a team member constantly beats deadlines, the temptation to offer a sarcastic remark such as, "As expected, So-and-so has beaten another deadline" belittles the actions that team member has taken.

A long, long time ago, when I was a software developer, I attended a team meeting at which the chief information officer (CIO) was making several announcements. One of the team members had solved a very difficult problem in a very creative manner, and he was rightfully proud of his unique accomplishment.

The CIO was also pleased by the breakthrough and proceeded to compliment the team member by saying, "I have no idea what drugs this guy was taking at the time of his breakthrough, but he has managed to create an excellent solution anyway." Following was the expected applause, but after the CIO left, the conversation turned to apologies by other team members for the CIO's belittling compliment.

This CIO may have thought he was offering a compliment with a twist of humor, but the truth is he belittled the accomplishment by insinuating the team member could not have done it on his own without the help of mind-altering drugs. In this case, the CIO should have simply offered his appreciation and congratulated the team member, as well as the whole team, for providing an environment that fosters such creative thinking.

The situation could have become a bonding force that, if properly used, would unite the team and rally them to continue to produce outstanding results. Instead, the team members became resentful and eventually only produced what was required to prevent termination and nothing more.

Another mistake in this vein is managers that patronize their team members. People do not like to be patronized. It is belittling, insulting, and projects the impression that you do not think much of them as individuals.

Regardless of what communications method you use with your team, do not be condescending. This is one of the quickest ways to lose your team's respect.

I once knew of a manager that had a pet peeve about spelling. Whenever a team member sent an e-mail to him that contained misspellings, he would send it back to her, complete with a letter grade, such as "C-," and corrections with instructions on how to operate the spell checker.

The team quickly lost respect for this manager—not to mention that the manager's e-mails were generally loaded with misspelled words and incorrect word usage. It did not take long for the manager to lose credibility.

History has proven repeatedly that it is not just what you say that counts; it is also how you say it. The success of your argument critically depends on the manner in which you present it.

Balance Control

In the business world, change is happening at a record pace due to technology and competition. The pressure to produce at work is growing rapidly. The stress can become unbearable to some, and eventually, the pressure will build to a point that it cannot be contained. That is the point when employees quit, productivity falls, morale sinks, and the pressure continues to build.

To paraphrase an old adage, all work and no play makes the office a dull place. Most people spend more that 33 percent of their day at work. The other 66 percent is usually spent taking care of family matters, bills, home repairs, and sleeping, so we can wake up the next day and do it all again. This creates a tremendous amount of stress, and that stress is like the pressure building in a pressure cooker. When enough pressure builds, the pressure will cause a catastrophic explosion.

Garson Kanin, a famous author and director, once said, "There are thousands of causes for stress, and one antidote to stress is self-expression. That's what happens to me every day. My thoughts get off my chest, down my sleeves, and onto my pad."

As Garson Kanin so eloquently points out, the antidote to stress is self-expression. This is such a simple method to relieve stress because it is the easiest thing for your employees to do. BE THEMSELVES! Let them tell a joke; let them laugh; let them waste some company time. Research has shown that the average child laughs about three hundred times a day, while the average adult laughs about twenty times a day, and most of that is outside of the work environment. As the pressure to work harder, produce more and be faster, and be more creative builds more and more stress, you must let your employees release some of that pressure in a controlled constructive manner.

I can hear you now. "Since when is wasting company time constructive?" This is a very good question, and the answer may surprise you.

Stress is not only harmful to your physical and metal health; it destroys creativity. Depending on your specific job, this can be devastating. For example, a computer programmer, artist, or engineer may spend over 90 percent of his time being creative, and he cannot create while stressed out. This translates into lost revenue because of increased sick days being taken, and excessive breaks that are truly non-productive.

Research has shown that laughter stimulates the immune system, increases endorphins, and reduces stress. In the workplace, humor and fun, in general, can increase productivity and improve team building.

I have worked on many teams in my career, and I can honestly say that the most productive and creative teams were the ones that were not looking over their shoulders to see if the boss was coming. They openly played and had fun, and 85 percent of the time, the answer to some problem was realized during those periods of what I like to call "productive play."

Early in my career, when I was an information systems manager, we had a team of programmers that were creating some innovative technology. Stress at times was high; deadlines were tight. But just before the maximum pressure point was reached, one of the programmers would shout out, "Key-ball." At that point, everyone simply dropped what he or she was doing and started playing a game they devised that involved tossing a foam rubber brick at each other, in an attempt to hit the opponent's keyboard.

The programmers had even written a program that they would run on their computers to keep score.

Each row of keys on the keyboard had a corresponding point value. The object was to defend your keyboard from the foam brick. The person with the lowest score, which translated to the least number of hits on his keyboard, was the winner. When one of the screens reached a predetermined level, the game was over.

The stress was relieved, the programmers renewed, and the ideas started flowing again. Many times during these "Key-ball" games, the programmers would be talking about problems they were having; the others would give their opinions on how to resolve the issue. Often, the game would never reach the predetermined score, as the programmers had stopped playing in favor of collaboration on an issue.

To this day, I have not found a more finely tuned team as that. The camaraderie, the team building, the productivity were more than any manager could expect from his team.

It is important, however, to keep in mind that not all humor is beneficial. Research has shown that there is a difference between how negative and positive humor affects us physically and emotionally. It is therefore important to enforce positive humor in the workplace. Humor that is racist, ageist, or cynical is generally negative and should be discouraged at all times.

The interesting fact about some forms of humor is that, as a manager or team leader, some forms of humor will be off limits to you, while team members can have more interaction. For example, two employees at the same employment level such as senior programmers can easily use playful insults while interacting with each other. However, should the same *playful insult* come from their superior, it could easily be interpreted as an insult.

It should also be noted that some people like to hang out together after work. As a manager, take care not to fall prey to the temptation to show your employees that you can be just as fun loving as the next person. Doing so can easily be viewed as permission to continue the rowdy behavior first thing Monday morning.

The bottom line is that humor in the workplace that helps reduce stress will help your team be more productive and creative. I am not saying that you need to turn your office into the next comedy workshop; after all, there are deadlines to meet and schedules to keep. However, you do not have to break up every group that looks like they may be having a good time. Let the team play a little. As British novelist Roald Dahl once said, "A little nonsense now and then is relished by the wisest men." Just balance the amount of control you demonstrate over your team and give them a break occasionally.

Flexibility of Style

A well-formed team is comprised of skilled individuals, each with his own style. Each team member has been developing his own style from the moment he was born. Each individual's style is unique and is a result of his creative abilities, and these abilities and skills are why he is part of your team.

Do not try to change any of your team members' style. It is theirs, and it is part of them. You can help manage their style and try to guide them gently toward methods that are more efficient, but you should not change them. Doing so will simply offend them and make them less effective.

Even if you could change the style of each of your team members, the result would be a group of like-minded robots simply following orders. If this is what you want, then perhaps you should consider a career in the military.

If any style needs to change, it will be yours as the team leader. This is not to say that you should bend to every whim of your team; after all, you have your own style as well, and in time, your team will adjust to your style of doing things. What I am talking about has more to do with tolerance of your team's way of doing things.

It is easier for one individual to change his style for the benefit of the team than to sacrifice the team's creativity simply to please the team leader. The character Spock best said it in his death scene in *Star Trek II*, "The needs of the many outweigh the needs of the few or the one."

In 1977, the Naval Submarine Medical Research Lab in Groton, Connecticut conducted an extensive research project to evaluate leadership-style flexibility. During this study, command leaders altered their leadership styles depending on the situation. Several test groups were subjected to similar situations, but the command leaders varied their leadership style to determine what style worked best in various stress-inducing situations.

The study examined how subordinates perceived the various leadership styles, whether they felt the style was effective or ineffective, and how they perceived their coworkers at the time. The study found that the best management style is a flexible one.

In other words, the more stressful a situation becomes, the more your style must change to reduce stress in your team. Contrary to popular belief, standing over one of your team members who is trying to resolve an issue will not result in a faster resolution; in fact, the exact opposite is true. During times of high stress, when a quick resolution to a problem is required, adding to the stress by standing over, behind, or generally watching over the team member working on the resolution will actually slow the process and can cause additional problems.

So keep your style flexible and resist the urge to stand over your team members when a problem arises. It is best simply to approach the team, discuss the issues and the possible resolutions, then walk away, and let your team do their magic.

I think Elizabeth Barrett Browning, one of the most respected poets of the Victorian era, said it best, "What is genius but the power of expressing one's individuality." Let your team's genius emerge through self-expression. Be flexible in your style, and you will be rewarded with a team that feels trusted. In return, they will perform like the geniuses they are.

Taking One for the Team

Everybody makes mistakes. People generally want to do well; they want to succeed, learn, grow, and advance in their careers. Employees and managers alike learn from their mistakes as well as mistakes of others. They use the information gathered from the results of those mistakes to expand their understanding of how to perform various tasks better.

Sometimes, the mistakes can be huge—the loss of a customer, under bidding a project, resulting cost overruns, or the failure to plan for disasters that shut down the business for several hours. At times like these, many managers are quick to point blame. Poor planning by so-and-so or so-

and-so failed to tell me, or they may even try to stick the blame on one of their own team members, even if it was, in fact, that team member's fault.

Sure, your team may have had responsibility for performing some task, such as setting up an exhibit at a trade show or getting that package to someone the next day, but they forgot. That package was not shipped, or the display for the trade show was left at the office 1,500 miles away.

It is your team. They may have been responsible for the various project tasks, but ultimately, responsibility is yours—the team leader. I am not saying that your team's making a mistake is your fault; they did, and you should deal with it. However, when it comes to explaining to the CEO what happened, do not stand your team up in front of the firing squad while you stand to the side.

Take the bullet for the team! Stand in front of your team and accept the responsibility on their behalf. Doing so will demonstrate to your team that you are there to protect them, that you are part of the team, and that you are a *standup* person. Your team will thank you for it, even while you are taking disciplinary action with your team members. You will have earned their trust and their loyalty.

Motivating the Team

I was recently paging through the March 2006 issue of *Business 2.0*, which was titled "Best-Kept Secrets of the World's Best Companies." I found the cover story article intriguing. As I read each of the twenty-five *secrets,* I noticed one common factor of each of these hugely successful companies. Each one empowered its team, communicated with them, and encouraged them using positive reinforcement.

Some of the concepts were simple but important to nurturing the creative minds of their employees. It is important to remember that there are no set rules, no ten commandments of team motivation; each company must find what works for them.

The simplest was Google's concept of office graffiti. The article explained how Google provides white boards in common areas and allows office staff to contribute their own personal statements, cartoons, and slogans. Google has managed to foster an excellent method of office communication. Employees are free to express their thoughts at any time, on any subject.

This simple concept helps spark the imagination, allows self-expression, and encourages everyone to participate, building morale and creating a fun work environment.

This form of free expression makes it easy for management to get a handle on the current state of morale. If jokes are amusing, poems lighthearted, and ideas sound, then morale is good. However, if jokes become less frequent, doodles become expressions of dissatisfaction, or employee participation drops, then morale is down. This type of indicator allows management to gauge office pressure, like a needle on a thermostat.

People spend at least one-third of their waking hours at work. Their coworkers become their second family. If your employees are not happy, their creative process becomes disturbed, and they will no longer be productive. This can quickly become a self-fulfilling prophecy if you start pushing your employees to perform better. They become dissatisfied with the situation, making it even harder to concentrate.

Therefore, it is extremely important to keep your employees as happy as possible. A happy employee is a creative employee; a creative employee is a productive employee; and a productive employee is a profitable employee. Need I go on?

The obvious question now is how to motivate the team. Unbelievably, it starts with you. You need to set an example for your team by walking your talk. If you expect your employees to be on time, then you should be on time as well, and if you expect high standards from your employees, then you should hold yourself to the same high standards, if not higher.

A simple "thank you" or "good morning" to your team members can have a noticeable impact. Show interest in your team members, take the time to speak to them, and I do not mean about a project or task on which they are working. Talk to your team members, ask them how they are doing, and then listen to them. I once asked an employee how he was doing and found out more than I expected. He opened up and informed me of several personal issues with which he was dealing. This was valuable information for me. Had I not asked the question, I would never have known his problems, and, as a result, would not understand his reasons for poor performance.

Simply by understanding and offering a sounding board for him to get things off his chest, I was able to help my team member through a difficult time. I understood what was going on when he informed me he needed an extra half-hour at lunch or needed to leave work early. We were able to work out a mutual understanding and help him through his difficult time without adding to his problems—all because I asked how he was doing.

Let your team members know they make a difference and that their contributions are appreciated. Communicate to them clearly and do not assume they understand, simply because you think you are communicating. Take the time to discuss goals and plans with them to insure they understand.

Above all, help your team members to succeed. No one comes to work with the intention to fail. It is your responsibility to understand each of your team members' strengths and weaknesses and put him in a position that will make him successful. Then work with him to improve areas of weakness. This builds confidence, which, in turn, motivates your team.

Focus on People

Today's world is significantly different from years past. Today, work can take place nearly anywhere and everywhere. For many workers, being chained to a desk is outdated. Technology has allowed employees to join a corporate conference from poolside, or sales documents can be drafted and approved as you enjoy the view from 30,000 feet while crossing the country in record time.

Successful organizations that deal in the global market have retired the old nine to five concept. Businesses realize that when it is five o'clock quitting time for them, the rest of the world is waking up and starting their day, having breakfast, or getting back from lunch. So why end your day when billions of potential customers are just starting theirs? A global market requires flexibility among its workers because work is done at different times, in different places, utilizing the latest collaborative technology.

In some cases, employees can be of more value at different times. For example, a database manager whose job is to perform routine maintenance on company databases may be wasted if he must simply sit at a desk and monitor the computer system database, then perform maintenance at night. Rather than wasting his time occupying a desk during the day, he can work from home at night performing his nightly maintenance while the other employees sleep.

Working virtually with a team that you rarely, if ever, see is becoming a frequent event in many organizations, and as such, you must learn to deal with diverse work groups. It is therefore paramount that you focus on the people to ensure peak performance.

Bureaucracy is not required when dealing with employees. Regardless of the work force's location—at home, at the airport, or in the office—you must avoid creating a bureaucracy. Avoid forms that take a week to fill out or complex methods for obtaining approvals that shift the focus away from the people and onto the organization.

In successful companies, there must be consequences for underachieving as well as recognizable rewards for meeting or exceeding expectations. By now, you are saying that this is all great and wonderful, but how do we do this? Honest feedback about how each team member and the team are performing is key. I have found that a simple "T" chart that lists three or four positive comments, as well as two or three areas that need improvement over the coming year, can be the best form of feedback.

In today's turbulent economic times, managers need to do more than batten down the hatches. They need to make sure their teams are on the right track, regardless of the external backdrop in which they work. Leaders who do this are reliably more successful, and their companies consistently have better results.

Beyond Goals

Goal setting is important in completing any task or project. In the case of a project, the goal is to complete the project to the customer's satisfaction, within a predetermined budget, and within a predetermined period.

In the case of personal goals, people tend to set their goals too low, which is usually a result of past failures. People tend to set their goals lower, so they become more achievable. The problem with this method is we tend to keep setting goals low. We become shortsighted and aim for those short-term goals.

The key to success, both yours and your teams, is to set your goals high—the higher, the better. If you would normally set a goal to become a department manager, then aim higher; set your goal to become the company president. If your goal already is to become the company president, then aim for chairperson of the board.

This is exactly what I did early in my career, and I did not even know it. I had an interview for the position of software development manager. I was rather nervous waiting in the reception area, thinking of how to handle various questions, making sure my shirt was neat, and the tie was straight. I was thinking about my posture and what position I would sit in while being interviewed—about all the usual things a young inexperienced up-and-comer would think.

I remember to this day, being led into the chief information officer's (CIO) office for the interview. The gentleman was well-dressed and radiated total confidence in his position and his teams. He was the type of person to whom you just felt comfortable speaking.

I sat down in my predetermined position, looked him straight in the eye, and waited for his first question. He paused, looked around, and then asked, "So what are your goals?" The obvious answer would have been to tell him how I wanted to use my talents to be the best software development manager I could be—how I wanted to learn more and advance within the department. That is not what I said. To this day, I still do not know why I said what I said, but I looked him in the eye and said, "I want your job!"

I froze! I thought the interview was over at that point. I did not know what to expect, but I was not nervous. In fact, I was still rather comfortable. After all, it was an open-ended question, and my answer was honest. I became more relaxed, as he continued to ask questions. I knew I had impressed him with my bold statement because his questions started to relate more to higher management than to software development.

At the end of the interview, we shook hands and I departed. I did not know what would happen next. I figured I would not get the job. His questions did not even relate to software development, and I figured that was it; I blew it.

A few days passed and still no call. I decided to call them and ask if they had selected anyone yet. As expected, I was informed that they had filled the position. "I knew it," I said to myself. I hung up the phone and continued my employment search.

About two hours later, the phone rang. It was the last place with whom I had interviewed. My mind started to race with thoughts of what must have happened. Their new hire changed his mind, and I was next on the list, or they changed their mind and decided I was the best man for the job. A million things shot through my mind in those first moments of the call. However, what they asked me never even crossed my mind at that point. I was speechless!

I was informed that the software development manager's position, in fact, had been filled, but the information systems director who interviewed me wanted to know if I would consider the position of Director of Software Development. I would report directly to the CIO, and the software development managers would report to me. I took the job!

After I hung up the phone, I thought about it and realized that my opening remark set the tone for the interview. If I had simply stated my goal was to get the job or be a software development manager, then the interview would have gone in that direction. However, I set my goal high, and that impressed the CIO. He saw that I was on a mission for success, and because of my comment, “I want your job,” I set the premise for his questions.

As the CIO, he is naturally looking for motivated, knowledgeable people to run the department, so my answer triggered his mind to think about his own replacement. This caused him to alter the interview based on his need rather than my need for a job.

Help your team establish goals that aim high. Encourage them to do everything they can to achieve those goals, even if that means leaving the company. Sure, you will have to replace them, but if they are not happy in their position and have no hope of achieving their goals working for the company, then how productive are they going to be? Les Brown, a renowned motivational speaker and author once said, “Shoot for the moon. Even if you miss it, you will land among the stars."

Inclusion and Participation

Humans have an inherent need to be included. From the moment a child is born, he wants to be needed, included in everything; he wants to be loved.

Employees are no different; they want to be needed. They want to be “in the loop.” By being in the know, employees feel comfortable and secure, and this eases their stress. However, when an office environment includes closed meetings, secret memos, and confidential meetings with supervisors and managers, employees become very uneasy. They feel threatened, and rumors start to fly. When an employee feels insecure, productivity drops, and ideas slow to a trickle as each employee begins to hoard information in hopes of adding value to his job to increase his job security.

Inclusion is a key element in creating a high-performance organization. To foster inclusion requires communication strategies that must be tailored to each organization. By promoting employee participation and encouraging inclusion through unified communications, organizations can enjoy increased productivity and reduce costly turnover in volatile times.

I remember one company I worked for early in my career where communications was non-existent. Rumors filled the hallways, and gossip was the norm at lunch.

In one particular situation, management had started a series of high-level meetings. Managers were called in, questioned, and then informed not to speak to anyone about the meeting. The rumor mill was buzzing with talk of layoffs, pay cuts, and anything else the employees could conjure up.

After a while, employees started to jump ship. They were resigning left and right in anticipation of massive layoffs. In response, management sent out informal e-mails to the employees, encouraging them to hold steady, that everything was fine, and the company was financially stable. The rumors increased along with resignations as employees took the informal e-mail as nothing more than propaganda. Eventually, the meetings ended, the dust of the mass exodus settled, and management made their announcement.

Management had been evaluating improvements to the health benefits, the compensation and merit increase policies, and relocation to a new, more spacious office only a few blocks away. Management announced that the large number of employees that felt they had to leave to find other employment disturbed them. The announcement went on to state that management felt it was necessary to keep the meetings secret so as not to build up the employees' expectations for the increase in benefits, in the event they decided not to make the changes.

This is a classic example of lack of inclusion. Had management simply informed the employees from the beginning what they were doing, the rumors would have never started, the mass exodus would never had happened, and productivity would never have dropped.

If your goal is productivity, then nothing can replace clear communication to keep your team productive. On the other hand, if your intention is to sabotage the team, then lack of communication will accomplish your goal twice as fast. Take the time to include your employees; if not directly, at least make them aware of what is happening. The lack of inclusion within an organization is directly proportional to the level of misunderstanding.

Training

One of the most effective methods of boosting an employee's morale and solidifying a sense of commitment in your team members is to shore up the professional development and training programs. Most team members enjoy the opportunity to receive additional training or develop as professionals. Lack of training is one of the quickest ways to develop morale problems and leave team members feeling unappreciated.

Even if your education budget is tight, you can still find economical ways to fund additional training. In today's world of on-line connectivity, there are on-line courses or computer based training (CBT). Even reimbursing team members for textbooks or creating your own library of books that your team can use are viable methods of providing additional training.

I once worked in a team environment where multiple team members wanted to take similar training, but the budget would not permit all team members to take the same courses. The solution was to allow each team member to choose a single area in which to obtain training. Once a team member completed his training, he would hold a series of team meetings and train his fellow team members. In this manner, the team was able to leverage their team structure to obtain additional training that would not have been possible any other way.

This method works best if the courses each team member attends are also available as CBT. This allows the company to build a library of training courses that all can use and provides a team member with formal training to assist the others should they have questions while completing the CBT.

Dealing with Conflicts

Conflict is an unpleasant fact in a team. Even when the team shares a common goal, its members will have different points of view and ideas about how to reach those goals.

Each team member brings with him a wealth of knowledge, experience, and ideas. With all those ideas, members of the team are going to have differences in opinion on how best to solve a problem. In many cases, this clash of ideas generally works itself out, the parties involved manage to arrive at a consensus, and a plan forms.

Ideas are personal; they are expressions of you, and team members can become passionate about their ideas. So much so, that in some cases, people can take rejection of an idea personally, and as a result, they will dig in and stand firm. When this happens, it can divide a team and discourage the expression of conflicting views. Members may begin to keep their ideas to themselves, afraid of causing new conflicts or fanning the flames of an old one.

The most productive teams are those that can walk the fine line of having differences and finding a way to work through them. Technologists, for example, are generally eager to learn and explore their colleagues' ideas and methods of thinking. In these teams, differences are not a hindrance, but a valuable tool that each member uses to refine his own ideas. These teams will bounce ideas off each other, and as a result, each member will refine his own ideas and concepts while the members interact.

The critical issue is how to guide the team into productive channels, have the team embrace differences, and resolve issues effectively. To resolve conflicts, you must listen to each side of the issue so that each member will at least feel he has been fairly heard, and he should be willing to support the team's decision. Unfortunately, not all conflicts are easily resolved and may require further exploration.

A Solution

One solution I have used in the past is rather simple, and if done right, can actually help build the team. First is the creation of the decision rules. Rules depersonalize disputes and undermine the *us-versus-them* mentality that can slow down the process, and rules help speed up the process. Decision rules are generally easier for a team to decide on and are easier to hammer out than the final decision.

Once the rules have been established, the group is divided into two groups of three to five members, with each group representing one point of view. The members of each group do not necessarily have to agree with the point of view of the group they have been assigned. In fact, it is best if each group has members representing both sides of the issue. Having both sides of the issue represented by a team that is assigned the task of supporting a single side of the issue causes the team members to feel less compelled to represent their own interests. As members of each group become more invested in the work, they become less emotionally linked, and they approach the issue with less passion.

Each side must then state its position on the issue and list all assumptions underlying its position. Once this is done, the members should step back and re-examine their ideas, beliefs, and the information that has led them to their present position.

Each group should then analyze the assumptions according to truth and importance. They will ask two questions of each assumption:

1. How certain are we that this is true?

2. How important is the assumption to the outcome?

Thorough discussion of these two questions as they are posed to each of the assumptions will give team members insight into the thoughts of their colleagues, allowing them to rethink the problem and discover the underlying issues. When each group feels they have sufficiently analyzed all the assumptions, the teams reconvene to review their findings. In most cases, both sides have reassessed their positions and are near agreement.

How does focusing on the assumptions help the group target the problem? Instead of examining a thousand reasons that support their opposing positions, members focus on a dozen key sub-issues. By analyzing the truth and relevance of the assumptions, the precise area of disagreement can be identified and resolved.

By the time this exercise has ended, the parties involved will walk away with a better understanding of the issues, and they will understand that they started with an incomplete picture of the situation.

The Facilitator

As with most conflict resolution techniques, assumption analysis has its advantages, and the team leader can easily perform it. However, it works best if you obtain the assistance of an outside facilitator. The outside facilitator can easily be anyone from within the company that does not have a direct link to the project, or it can be a professional facilitator contracted for this purpose.

By obtaining a facilitator, the team leader is freed from having to worry about being fair and can spend more time listening. Additionally, if the team leader is a department manager or other high-level manager, then members may feel intimidated, whereas with an outsider, they can speak candidly.

Conflict resolution does not always resolve the problem at hand, and assumption analysis is no exception. It is possible that once the exercises outlined here are complete, the members of each position may have actually established a stronger case for each of their positions, and the result could be two valid options to resolve the same issue.

In situations such as this, a decision has to be made as to which solution to use. You can make an executive decision that should have been established in the rules earlier. The other alternative is to assign the decision to the team to make the determination based on a set of predefined rules that are designed for the benefit of the company rather than any particular viewpoint.

A Job Well Done

Recognizing a team member for performing a job well may seem trivial to some managers, but in a recent survey, only 35 percent of employers actively recognize when their team members contribute on an individual basis. Sure, many companies often congratulate the team for a successful quarter or achieving an established milestone, and most of those congratulatory remarks have traditionally been focused toward the sales department.

The sales department is not the only team in your organization that deserves congratulations; in fact, you should make it a point to identify individuals from within the organization to be singled out for special congratulations when it is warranted.

They say there is no "I" in team, but the reality is that regardless of the team, it is comprised of individuals, and the individuals that have made outstanding contributions need to be recognized as individuals.

Praise Publicly

How important is it to praise the performance of your team members? If you want to turn a mediocre team into a magnificent one, it is essential!

Everyone wants recognition for his or her hard work. From the moment we are born, we are striving for recognition from our parents, a friend, a teacher, and eventually our employer and colleagues. To receive recognition means we have value as a person, and this makes us feel good about ourselves, which re-enforces our continued efforts of achievement.

The web is full of "I hate my boss" Web sites, where frustrated employees spend countless hours complaining about their bosses and offering suggestions about how they would handle issues. Interestingly, most people are looking for appreciation of their work, recognition of a job well done, followed closely by communication, with job security in third place while money or compensation is relatively low on the list.

The interesting part is that all three of the top issues that employees want are intricately related. Public recognition in itself communicates to the individual as well as the whole team that they have value, and you appreciate them. This, in turn, gives the person being recognized, as well as the whole team, the feeling that his job is secure. Even the most troublesome team member will respond well to public praise and, in many cases, can cause the team member to continue to improve, becoming a valuable team member.

Using a method borrowed from marketing called perception-preceding-reality, I have seen team members that otherwise would have been terminated make a complete behavioral turnaround. While the roots of this concept are primarily from marketing, it is an excellent term to describe a method for altering a team member's behavior who is not always a team player.

By taking the time to seek out actions and behaviors of borderline team members that you can praise publicly, you will effectively reinforce positive behavior in that employee. This reinforcement will play to the employee's self-esteem, and with time, positive behavior will dominate his actions. The idea is that the positive feedback will reinforce positive behavior, as well as the team member's transition to being a team player, which will ultimately catch up with the perception.

Mary Kay Ash, the founder of Mary Kay Cosmetics once said, "There are two things people want more than sex and money, and they are recognition and praise."
However, before you run out and start praising your team for every little thing they do, take care in what you praise and how often. Praise works best in moderation, so use it sparingly. If you start praising every little thing, eventually your praise becomes nothing more than an annoyance, as your team will quickly see that the praise is not sincere.

Employees need praise, like plants need sunlight. Just like a tree spreads its branches to absorb more sunlight, without praise, your employees will leave in search of praise.

Non-Monetary Awards

Employee recognition is not a fad or a temporary tool used to do something nice for your employees. Employee recognition is an ongoing communication tool that rewards positive contributions and should be performed on a regular basis.

Even if a project fails, the team members may have performed outstandingly and deserve to be recognized for their efforts, especially after a failed project. You may be thinking, "Why reward failure?" Well, you are not. If a project failed, other extenuating circumstances—poor project conception, poor budgeting, or unreasonably shifting demands by a customer—may have caused the failure.

You must look at the individuals that make up the team and award those that contributed. The project may have failed, but the individuals may have made other outstanding breakthroughs that can help in other projects.

As long as team members gave their best effort, and those efforts can be utilized elsewhere, then the project is not a complete failure, and those team members should be recognized.

When a team member completes a project, and he has performed well, it is important to recognize his efforts to build his self-esteem and show him that his efforts were noticed. Even if only a few team members are recognized, it boosts morale for all team members so that they will enter their next project eager and ready to produce.

In fact, if the previous project failed, it is even more important to recognize team members. At the time of the project failure, team members may be second-guessing their actions. Did they do everything they could? Did they miss something? They become demoralized and feel a sense of failure that accompanies them to the next project. As a result, they take fewer risks, they become cautious, and produce less.

Recognizing outstanding effort, even from a failed project, takes them off the hook, restores their confidence, and tells them that they were not to blame for the project failure. As a result, they will enter their next project free of the burden of past failures and will work even harder to make the next project a success.

So what type of award do you use to recognize your team? There are many ways to award team members.

Awards do not have to be monetary. They can be certificates of appreciation or something as simple as a pat on the back and the acknowledgement of a job well done. Non-monetary awards are much easier to distribute and can do more for the team as a whole, even if only one member receives the award. Most employees recognize outstanding ideas when they see them and want to see those that have performed well be rewarded. It reassures them that you are watching, noticing what they do, and that you recognize their value as team members.

It must be stressed that because of the ease in handing out non-monetary awards, the temptation to award every little action should be resisted. If you start handing out awards simply because you feel some team members have not had one, then that act will devalue the reward. It would not be fair to those that received the "Award for Outstanding Achievement" for developing a method of reducing costs and saving the company millions to have another team member receive the same award because he has not made a mistake for a while, even though it may be a big achievement for that employee.

The point is to make sure the award retains its value, and it is only presented when it is truly deserved. By maintaining the award's credibility, it provides the other team members with something to strive for, so they can set goals.

To ensure the value of non-monetary awards, draft a set of rules that will govern that award. Set the award's criteria, and make sure each team member is aware of the rules. This allows him to understand how important the award is and respect the team members that receive the award because he will know what it took to get the award.

Listed here are a few ideas of awards that I have seen used successfully in several organizations.

On-the-spot award. This can be a simple gesture or a small merchandise award that is granted as a means to recognize employees for those day-to-day efforts, which contribute in a special way to getting the job done. This could be almost anything from a pat on the back and simple acknowledgement to a gag type award that is part of a running joke in the office.

At one company I worked, the team created their own award. Someone on the team created a simple award out of a few broken circuit boards mounted on a wooden base. The team gave the award to any other team member that made a major breakthrough on the current project. Once a member received the award, he would add his name and the date to the base and hang onto the award. When another team member made a significant discovery or contribution to the project, the current award holder would pass the award on to the next deserving recipient.

This concept worked wonders for team spirit. Eventually, the team had even developed awards for team members that totally messed up. With these awards, a team member would be stuck with it until someone else made a major blunder.

You may be wondering why anyone would create an award like that. The answer is simple. The award acted as a grounding post for stress. By creating an award and placing the name of each recipient on the award with the date, it reminded each member of the team that he or she is not alone. Others have made mistakes, and it is ok to make mistakes. Some mistakes were so big, however, that passing of the award was sometimes delayed for quite a while. Other times, the offending member would simply get up and take the award in acknowledgement of the offense.

It should be noted you do not want to create this type of award as a team leader. The team should create these types of awards on their own. However, if you see that your team has created such an award, take comfort that your team has bonded and trust each other enough to be able to expose themselves to such peer review. It means you have done well in selecting your team members.

Time off award. This award allows managers to grant employees time off from duty without loss of pay or charge of leave. These awards are normally used as an alternative to special act or service awards. With this type of award, you may grant as little as an extra half-hour or full hour for lunch, or you could give someone a day or two off.

In the past, I have let employees go home an hour earlier simply because they have been working so hard on a project. Other times, I have told team members to take a three-day weekend on the company; they could choose Friday or Monday to take off.

Sometimes dedicated team members can be burnt out working on a project. Keep an eye on your team members, looking out for anyone that may be burnt out, and give him or her a day off. If your team is burnt out, they are of no use anyway. They will simply sit there killing time, becoming more frustrated and more burnt out. You may as well give them a day off every now and then to prevent burnout. After all, you are paying them either way, so you may as well get the most out of that wasted day and let them recharge.

Granted, this is not exactly a non-monetary award, as it does promote paid time off. You may want to clear this type of award with your supervisor or human resources department first.

Certificates of appreciation. These certificates are granted to employees or non-employees who have made outstanding contributions or who have performed significant services to the department. As stated earlier, establish a set of guidelines for these awards, and stick to those guidelines.

Resist the temptation to present awards to everyone simply because he has not received an award or it has been a while since he received one. This devalues the award for everyone and, eventually, becomes nothing more than cubical wallpaper.

Experience certificates. Instead of the traditional gift certificates that some employers present team members for outstanding performance, you could present outstanding performers with vouchers for ski school, golf school, spa retreats, or even racecar driving school.

Serial acts of appreciation. This is a great motivator that not only gets teams motivated but keeps them performing in many cases out of curiosity, because they never know what to expect or when the act will occur. The popular restaurant chain, The Olive Garden, surprised top workers by sending them a different reward everyday for seven days straight as reported by the *Orlando Business*

Journal. One day, workers received a letter of congratulations from top managers; the next day, they received chocolates, then movie tickets, restaurant gift certificates, Olive Garden gift cards, denim shirts, and, finally, wristwatches.

Fringe Benefits

There was a time that fringe benefits were commonly available to employees, but in today's cost-cutting, bottom line-oriented business world, employers are keeping a watchful eye on fringe benefits to the point where many employees no longer understand what a fringe benefit is anymore.

First, let me say this about fringe benefits. They are a great way to tell your team that they matter! It is important to make the distinction between a fringe benefit and a bonus. A bonus is generally a monetary reward designed to reward positive behavior and is a method for controlling employees, as discussed elsewhere in this book. A fringe benefit, on the other hand, is a little something extra, regardless of past performance or expectation of future performance.

Most teenage girls working at the mall for the summer understand the concept of fringe benefits even though they may not know the term. What they do know is that by working at their favorite clothing outlet, they not only get a paycheck, but they also get an employee discount on any purchases from the store. To your average teenage girl, this is a great fringe benefit for working at the mall. They cannot only get a paycheck, but when they spend every penny they earned at the store they work for, their money goes further. Teenage economics at its best!

I was at Ben and Jerry's Waterbury, Vermont manufacturing plant for a tour many years ago. I observed how they mixed the receipts for the various ice cream combinations, how they processed the fresh fruit that goes in many of the mixes, and how much detail they paid to quality control. In addition to all these things, I also noticed how much time they spent on the quality of their employees. The employees were happy and enjoyed what they did. I was informed that each employee is provided three free pints of ice cream per day. I immediately calculated that that comes to almost 137 gallons of ice cream per year. Hey, if you have kids and/or love ice cream, this is a great fringe benefit.

Employee discounts and free products aside, many employers offer other great fringe benefits such as tuition money for higher education, low interest or no-interest loans, or free movie tickets for the family. These fringe benefits do not have to be company product based either, many companies provide movie tickets, prepaid gift cards, or any number of low cost items merely to say thank you. The point is, the employees appreciate, but do not expect, the fringe benefits.

It is important to understand the fringe benefits are provided to employees regardless of their performance. Yes, even the troubled employees get them. Do not dangle the fringe benefit in front of any of your employees in hopes that it, in some way, will motivate them to perform better. Doing so will backfire on you, productivity will drop, and you will lose any trust or respect they have for you.

I have found out from my own experiences that fringe benefits should especially be given to those employees that may be performing poorly or may be in a slump, as it is the quickest method for revitalizing them, getting them out of a slump, and telling them they are appreciated.

Fringe benefits are intended to help boost morale and give employees the emotional pat on the back that everyone needs from time to time. Done correctly and just often enough, you will find that offering fringe benefits is a great way to keep your team creative, motivated, and healthy.

Spousal Rewards

It is a fact that some team members will get married or have boyfriends or girlfriends. Often, weekends are set aside for personal relationships—a baseball game with the kids, dinner and a movie with a spouse, or a trip out-of-town to just get away from it all.

Sometimes, duty calls. That server needs an upgrade, the financial reports have to be done by Monday, or that out-of-town meeting just cannot wait. Because of this intrusion into that personal relationship, your team members may get the silent treatment for canceling a weekend away or be dealing with any number of issues because of having to perform extra work.

Sure, you may not see it as extra work, but spouses often do. They sometimes cannot understand why someone else cannot fix the server or complete the reports. As a result, your team member may not have his heart in it 100 percent. He may be thinking about how to patch up the relationship or how to deflect the blame. The bottom line is that your team member is not happy; or you might say, "If the spouse isn't happy, the team member isn't happy!"

I have found that giving your team member's significant other a reward can go a long way. A gift card for the mall, or anything else you have discovered through your team members that he or she may like, will work. You may even want to ask your employees what their spouses' interests are.

I once worked for a company that sent a team member's spouse to a weekend spa while her husband worked. I later heard she had asked him to work more weekends, so she could go to the spa more often. In this case, the husband was able to concentrate on the task, secure in the knowledge that his wife was happy, and there would be no *fall-out* upon returning home.

De-motivation

How would you like to have the most unproductive team possible, reach new lows and show everyone how to waste time and money? If this is what you want, then stop reading right now!

De-motivation is the easiest thing in the world to do to your team. Unfortunately, for some reason, many managers spend a tremendous amount of time raising de-motivation to an art form without realizing it. Crushing enthusiasm, creating resentment, demoralizing, and betraying trust are easy things to do if you do not take the time to show your team that you appreciate and trust them.

There are more motivational resources available today than any other time in history. However, despite this dazzling array of motivational solutions available, more and more people are claiming that they hate their jobs.

How is it possible, you ask? Poor management is the reason—managers who are too self-promoting, too eager to claim credit, or too quick to point blame. These managers do not understand the importance of their team; they view the team as a group of servants with the task of making the manager look good.

These de-motivational managers have only their own personal employment and advancement in mind. These managers tend to give assignments or tasks that will keep team members looking busy but will not allow anyone to claim credit for anything.

These managers tend to inform their team to clean up the area when the CEO is going to show up, or they are concerned with making sure everyone looks busy. They do not understand that a valuable team that is trusted and has had responsibility delegated to them will naturally be busy and look responsible.

Many de-motivational managers will constantly try new techniques and methods in a futile attempt to motivate their team. Some of the techniques tried may actually work, but these managers lack the ability to follow through with the techniques. They quickly drop it or move onto a new method assuming the last method failed without giving it ample time to show results. These managers continuously fall back into old habits, too concerned with their own image and the reflection of the team's lack of motivation on them as managers. Dwight David Eisenhower once said, "Motivation is the art of getting people to do what you want them to do because they want to do it."

De-motivation is easy; anyone can de-motivate a team—self-preservation, lack of compassion for others, selfishness, and ego are easy for many. Only a true leader can move beyond these de-motivational tendencies and motivate his team through trust, compassion, and concern for the team's wellbeing.

Inconsistency

One of the quickest ways to destroy enthusiasm, morale, and creativity at work is inconsistency—inconsistency in applying rules, policies, and communications. If you single out one employee for excessive use of the Internet, while another employee is free to surf for personal use without any repercussions, then issues of favoritism will quickly spread. Granted, you may be enforcing company policy with your team members while the team leader of another team is more relaxed on the issue of Internet surfing. However, this sends a very negative message to all team members regardless of what team they are on.

When dealing with company policy, employees do not see a difference between one team and another. They view all employees of the company as one team with the same company policy, and they would be correct in making that assumption as well. In the areas involving company policy, it is your responsibility as the team leader to communicate with other team leaders to establish consistent use of company policy.

I have often been an advocate of turning matters such as Internet usage and any other area covered by the company policies over to the company's human resources department. Let the HR department enforce company policy for all employees equally. With that said, let's focus on your team now.

Inconsistency within the team will also destroy enthusiasm, morale, and creativity. You must establish efficient communications and team policies and enforce them consistently. As team leader, it is your responsibility to communicate the team's policies to other departments and enforce those policies. You cannot make exceptions to the policies and still maintain consistency.

Here is a perfect example of this type of inconsistency that I have experienced many times in the field of information technology. Upon taking over a company's IT department, I discovered that the IT people were receiving calls from employees with requests to resolve various issues with which the IT department rarely had anything to do.

After speaking to the CEO about the issue, he assured me that he would make it clear to the staff that they should contact the support department for all problems. He then informed me that once the policy went into effect that I should notify him immediately if the problem continued. I figured my problem was solved at this point.

A few days later, he called me, and the first thing out of his mouth was, "I know I'm supposed to call the support department, but can you take care of this issue for me?" I calmly informed him that I was still having an issue with one of the employees not following policy.

In the real world, however, there will always be exceptions to the rule. If your CEO, president, or VP of finance, for example, has an issue, do not allow him to go directly to your team members without first clearing it with you. Enforce your team policies.

If you are inconsistent with goals, answering questions, or enforcing team policies, your team will simply tune you out. They will label you as inept, and anything you say or do after that will be suspect. They will anticipate your next reversal, which if by chance you do, will confirm their assumptions, and you will find yourself in a hole in which you may not be able to climb out.

Do not Aim for or Demand Perfection

What is perfection? I remember my teacher telling me that "Practice makes perfect," and I also remember whenever I made a mistake on my homework, the teacher telling me, "It's okay; no one is perfect."

Is perfection achievable? Can an imperfect human achieve perfection in anything he does? I personally do not think so. He may come close but achieve absolute perfection, no! So, if man cannot achieve perfection, then why is it that so many managers demand it from their teams?

The truth is that not all managers demand perfection from their teams. The successful manager understands that done is better than perfect and encourages his teams to complete projects with care and an eye for detail, knowing that no project will ever be perfect.

This is because perfection is a subjective term. Everybody has a different perception of what is perfect. If you, as a manager, are going to demand that a project be perfect, then what are you really asking your team to do? You are asking them to do the job to achieve your version of perfection. Since your idea of perfection is naturally going to vary from their idea of perfection, then you are asking them to take a wild guess at what you want.

If you aim for or demand perfection from your team, you will be disappointed, morale will drop, deadlines will be missed, and you and your team will appear disorganized, unprofessional, and incapable of delivering projects in a timely fashion.

Perfection has long been the subject of controversy. Salvador Dali once said, "Have no fear of perfection—you will never reach it."

Micromanaging

Everyone hates being micromanaged. Micromanaging your team members makes them feel like they are not trusted, respected, or thought highly of by their own manager. These feelings eat away at employee morale.

Micromanagers, like many addicts, alcoholics, rage-aholics, fanatics, etc., are the last people on the planet to recognize their addiction is in controlling others. The compulsion to look over employees' shoulders has nothing to do with being meticulous or careful; it has everything to do with control.

If you are a micromanager, your employees have a name for you, for example, ruler, extremist, bureaucrat, tyrant, bully, persecutor, or tormenter. And trust me; those are the nice names. People who micromanage do so because they are the ones who feel unsure and self-doubting.

An unmistakable sign of micromanaging is continual mistrust, which simultaneously is the most distinctive feature of any micromanager. Micro-managers are generally suspicious, touchy, humorless, quick to take offense and slow to forgive, self-righteous, argumentative, and often litigious. They prefer to keep distance and avoid any intimacy; often, they seem tense, cold, and brusque. Micromanagers find causal connections everywhere; for them, nothing is coincidental. Overall, micromanagement is a pathological reaction of paranoia and associated feelings of insecurity and distrust.

An employee knows immediately when they are being micromanaged. However, a manager does not always recognize that he is micromanaging his staff.

Do you spend a measurable amount of time hand-holding employees? If so, then ask yourself if this person is capable of doing the job. Is there additional training that the person could receive that would free up your time?

Do you spend time telling people exactly what to do and how? If you do, try letting the employees find the answers themselves. Often, there are multiple solutions to most problems. You may find that another solution works just as well, if not better.

Do you spend a measurable amount of time overseeing particular projects? If you are spending too much time checking up on a project, perhaps you should simply organize a weekly status meeting. Let your team prove their capabilities. However, if you do not like the results presented at the status meeting, tell your team what you expect by the next status meeting, and let them do their job. It may take a few meetings to get noticeable results.

Do you find yourself irritated when others make decisions without consulting you? If you do, then ask yourself if it really matters in the end. Was the decision correct? If it was, then take comfort knowing that you trained your team well.

Sometimes, you need to let go of things and allow people to find their own way. Yes, they may make mistakes, but wonderful discoveries for new and better ways might be made as well. After all, history has shown repeatedly that most of the greatest discoveries have all been the results of mistakes.

Sure, it takes time in the short term to train the employees on how they need to do things, but it is worth the time commitment. You and your team members will benefit in many ways. You will end up with more time in your day to devote to more important matters, and your employees will be able to breathe easy knowing that you are not going to be hovering and micromanaging them to death—not to mention the improvement in morale from the employees feeling good about the fact that you actually believe in them!

Failure Happens

No one wants to fail, but from time to time, your team may fail. They may fail to meet a deadline, fail to anticipate various issues, in short, a project may fail for any number of reasons.

If you are not dealing with a project but some other task, it is also possible that a team member can make a mistake—a decimal in the wrong place, an incorrectly configured router, or a misplaced file. In short, errors happen for one reason or another, and the reason behind the error may be a valid reason that has exposed a flawed process, or it may be a simple careless mistake.

Most managers spend too much time trying to prevent failure by micromanaging various aspects of a project or task. They stand by in frustration as mistakes happen, and carelessness proliferates. They assume they must be more diligent in their control of the situation and enact controls that are more stringent, requiring more and more oversight. Eventually, the controls begin to choke out responsibility and accountability. It sounds counter intuitive, but the more control management enacts, the less responsibility team members have.

You may be asking how this is possible. Conventional wisdom is that more control means more care is taken, and errors in the workplace are reduced. Reality, however, is much different. The more rules and controls management enacts that require a team member to seek approval of other managers, the thinner the blanket of responsibility becomes.

In an overly controlled environment with multiple checks and balances, it becomes easy for someone to lay the blame elsewhere. If that planned upgrade fails, blame will be placed on those that approved the plan, claiming they should not have approved it, or they obviously did not look closely at the proposed plan. In other words, the more levels of approval that are required, the more the blame is distributed. However, when responsibility is on one individual or team to perform a task, knowing that if things go wrong, they will have to take responsibility for the decisions, the individual or team responsible is more likely to take extra care to ensure nothing goes wrong.

Now, I am not saying you should stop all approvals of projects or tasks. Some things will always require approval at some time or another, but care should be taken to define clearly where responsibility rests. Once you have established who is responsible, let them be responsible. Do not give them a chance to shift blame. If the task fails, it fails. Deal with it.

If you are going to jump in, in an attempt to prevent a disaster, only to realize the disaster happens regardless, then you have set yourself up for the blame because you have taken responsibility. You cannot take control and delegate the responsibility to someone else. To paraphrase Henry Kissinger, it is, after all, the responsibility of the expert to operate the familiar and that of the leader to yield to the experts.

Familiarity Breeds Contempt

Charles de Gaulle once said, "There can be no prestige without mystery, for familiarity breeds contempt." So, does familiarity breed contempt? The answer is a resounding yes! Many managers have had this concept drilled into them since their earliest days of MBA school and management training.

I remember my mother and many of my grade school teachers drilling this into me for as long as I can remember. I have also witnessed managers lose control, authority, and their effectiveness simply by becoming too familiar with their subordinates.

Most negative office politics are the result of too much familiarity. The TV show *The Office* is loaded with examples of what can happen when employees become too familiar. Familiarity leads to employee contempt regardless of how talented the manager may be. It is human nature to compare yourself to other people and question why a manager is worthy of a position of power.

At its core, the concept of *familiarity breeds contempt* is based on the idea that the more we know a supervisor on a personal level, the more likely we are to find fault with them. An example of this phenomenon is actors. It is played out on TV, day in and day out. A talented actor is speaking out for some wonderful organization and donating millions of dollars from his most recent film, while the public holds him in high regard for his charitable acts and superb acting simply because the public does not *know* him on a personal level.

Then the news is broadcast from coast to coast that the actor that everyone held in such high regard has a drug addiction, is a sex offender, or has political views that are so far to one side that he has created his own political position shared by a small faction of like-minded individuals. Instantly, the respect we had for him is gone and we feel betrayed, all because we learn something intimate about that actor's life.

I used the reference to actors, but this scenario has played itself out among musicians, politicians, and high profile executives from Adelphia Cable to Enron to WorldCom. There is no doubt in my mind that people the world over will continue to be disappointed in someone by becoming too familiar.

Personal disclosure and subordinate contempt

People often wonder how successful managers become so successful. People often speculate about them and often try to analyze them.

On the other side of the successful manager is the not-so-good manager, and most managers know why they are not the greatest managers. They know these managers inside and out, and in some cases, they know the managers better than the managers know themselves.

Why such stark differences? Well, the successful managers know how to keep their private lives private. They do not forge personal relationships with subordinates. On the other side of that are the not-so-great managers that forge relationships with subordinates; they talk too much and share their personal lives too freely. Successful managers and leaders are very careful only to disclose favorable personal details such as charitable acts or other information that they feel is beneficial to the organization and their teams.

Disclosure of politics and religion

Politics and religion are two of the most common catalysts for breeding contempt in the workplace. Once you make your religious or political views known to your subordinates, the damage is done. Many managers have lost credibility among their subordinates after polarizing their teams based on political or religious viewpoints.

When discussions of religion or politics arise, do not be pulled into them. In fact, try to discourage these types of conversations all together as nothing positive ever results.

Private corporations and over-familiarity

Employee contempt is often exacerbated in family-owned businesses where the owners' children may be taking over when their parents retire, often, without regard for their worthiness or ability to run the organization. Often, these children will begin working alongside other employees as they learn the business. However, these children are often promoted to higher and higher positions as rightful owners of the business as the family places them into key positions.

In cases such as this, the children tend to forge relationships with other coworkers. In the beginning, they may justify this behavior as "getting to know the workers" and the business, but this often backfires, as the co-workers tend to learn about the children of the owner on a personal level as well.

Non-family workers are often passed over for promotion in favor of the owners' children, as the children are promoted via the fast track. If the family members were not careful to guard their personal lives closely from their co-workers, the contempt can be amplified.

Discipline

Discipline in the workplace is a difficult task to perform for most team leaders, and as a result, many managers avoid it, hoping the problem will resolve itself. Other times, they avoid disciplining a team member by rationalizing that maybe it was a one-time thing and it will not happen again.

Then the unthinkable does happen. The employee makes the same error or crosses the line in such a way that discipline is inevitable.

The primary problem I have found is that most managers continue to refer to correcting a team member's action as discipline. Although employee discipline has its place in business, it should only be used in situations where other more positive methods have failed, and you are quickly approaching the possibility of termination. I believe that adopting a concept of coaching is a much more productive method with which to start and gradually move toward discipline if the situation warrants it.

Employees rarely respond positively to a true disciplinary session. They generally exit the session feeling disciplined and as a result, productivity will drop. They will be preoccupied thinking about the disciplinary session.

When a team member starts demonstrating behavior that needs to be dealt with, the fact is you both have a problem. The team member demonstrates unwanted behavior, and you have the problem of dealing with it. Therefore, by adopting a coaching attitude, you are effectively acknowledging that you both have a problem, and your desire is to help the team member deal with it, and you are willing to assist.

I have often found that in many cases, a team member may not have been aware that his actions were an issue. Often through coaching, you can make him aware of the issue and establish a plan to resolve the issue.

I remember having had a team member once that possessed complete mastery of his job. He often would put things off to the last minute knowing that he could quickly complete his tasks with plenty of time to spare. Because of this attitude, he tended to spend a lot of time working on projects that were of more interest. The problem was that many times he was holding up the project as people were waiting for him to complete his tasks. They knew the tasks would be completed on time, but they grew more and more frustrated by his lack of enthusiasm.

The time came to take action, and I was told he needed to be disciplined as his previous manager had done before. I therefore thought about it and decided just to talk to him about the issue rather than having a disciplinary session. I called him in and simply started the conversation with a simple question asking him how he was doing. The conversation gradually moved to project deadlines and completing tasks on time and eventually moved to the importance of completing projects as soon as possible and then working on the other, more interesting projects later.

As it turned out, he was under the impression, based on his previous discipline sessions, that he had to be more diligent in completing his project before the deadline. He assumed one or two days before that deadline was acceptable. Once I showed him the big picture and the effect his taking two weeks to complete a task that should take him two hours had on the team, he was open to discussing ideas as to how to resolve the issue.

We drafted a set of guidelines that he would follow when assigned a project. Because of that coaching session, we arrived at an acceptable solution that we both could live with, and he walked out of my office with a sense of accomplishment and a set of goals for advancing his career. It was a win-win situation.

Granted, not every situation that arises can be handled as a coaching session. Sometimes discipline in the form of a written warning, suspension, or termination is necessary. In this chapter, we will discuss several steps as we gradually move from coaching to discipline.

Counseling

It is a difficult situation when employee counseling is required. Often, it may seem easier simply to terminate the employee. However, you have invested a great amount of time and effort in training the employee, and it is possible that the employee's performance can be altered. Therefore, counseling is generally the first step in dealing with employee problems.

Counseling an employee is no different from any other project, and it requires a solid action plan. The plan must effectively address the employee's behavior in a positive manner so that his work performance improves and does not negatively affect the morale of the team.

Do not mistake disciplinary action with disciplinary counseling. They are two entirely different actions. Suspension or termination are examples of disciplinary action, whereas counseling unwanted behavior in an effort to improve work performance, while allowing the employee to understand what is expected of him, is disciplinary counseling.

It is always best to fix a problem at the onset rather than waiting for the situation to get out of control. That is where counseling comes in.

The most important aspect of disciplinary counseling is to save the employee's dignity so that he does not resent the disciplinary counseling. Discipline should be discreet and should avoid any embarrassment to the employee. Your goal is to collaborate with the employee to work and solve a mutual problem—the employee's unwanted behavior. Yes, it is a mutual problem and should be addressed as such.

I cannot stress it enough that employee discipline should never take place in the presence of other employees. The only exception to this would be if you wish to have a representative from your human resources department present to document the plan of action. Generally, I do not include the human resources department on a first-time counseling session.

Rather than laying down the law, so to speak, you should work to motivate your problem employee so he takes responsibility for improving his own work performance. Often, I have found that in first-time counseling sessions where motivation is the underlying issue, a good pep talk does an effective job at refocusing the employee.

As stated earlier, an effective plan of action is paramount in employee counseling. That plan should ensure that the employee understands what the problem is and what must be done to correct the problem. Your plan should be in writing and should detail exactly what happened, what the problem is, and what needs to be done to correct the issue, and like any other well-planned project, should have a deadline for correcting the issue.

Some issues simply cannot be changed overnight. As the old adage goes, "It is not easy teaching old dogs new tricks," and for employees, it may take some time and continued coaching until the unwanted behavior has been eliminated, so plan for this eventuality.

Make sure you have gathered as many facts and as much information as possible before you start counseling the employee. Doing so will help you during the discussion and may allow the employee to recall various situations and thereby become aware of his behavior. Facts are also difficult for the employee to deny and prevents the situation from becoming a *he said, she said* type of argument.

Your plan should also include a schedule to follow up with the employee after the counseling session so that the employee can receive feedback as to his progress in correcting the issue. This will ensure that the employee will not simply walk away from the session with a *thank goodness that's over with* attitude.

Follow-up also allows you to evaluate the employee's progress and perhaps offer additional encouragement. This can help relieve much of the tension that will result from the disciplinary discussion. If the employee is on the correct path, it can boost his morale knowing he is making progress and you are pleased with his new behavior. On the other hand, if you notice the employee is beginning to stray from the set course of action, it is possible he is simply falling into old habits, and these follow-up sessions can refocus his efforts on correcting the behavior.

Avoid using the follow-up sessions as additional disciplinary discussions. Doing so will cause the employee simply to think you are *out to get him*, and all past progress may be compromised. Additional disciplinary sessions, if needed, should not take place until the deadline discussed in the original disciplinary discussion has come and gone.

If after several of these follow-up sessions, you feel that your employee is not sincere, then it may be time to consider further action. However, if you feel that rehabilitation is still possible, then you may want to consider a series of projects designed to improve your employee's job performance.

These additional projects may be sending the employee back through your company's new employee training process, or partnering the employee with a colleague to gain further knowledge. Whatever process you decide on, the process should start as soon as possible.

Once the employee has completed the disciplinary project that you had laid out for him, you should have a final review of the employee's performance. If the performance has improved, and the unwanted behavior has been corrected, then no further action is required, and you and your employee can place the issue behind you. However, if there are still issues with the employee behavior, then it may be time for a more formal disciplinary action.

Focus on Specific Behavior Goals

Often, managers skim over and play down issues relating to employee behavior in an effort to make the employee more comfortable or not feel as if you are picking on him. Doing this is flat out wrong. It is patronizing and often makes the employee feel that the behavior is not a big deal and therefore does not warrant much consideration. In the end, this leads to more confrontation and additional disciplinary discussions. When discussing behavior issues, be as specific as possible in regards to the unwanted behavior. You do not have to be stern or overbearing, just conversational.

If the employee is neglecting a project or is not making much progress on a project, you will do much better in discovering the underlying issues in a calm conversational voice with the aim of discovering the true cause. Often this type of discussion will result in the discovery of issues of which you may not have been aware, and the employee simply did not realize or know how to handle the issue.

If, however, you choose not to take a conversational tone, it is likely the employee will quickly slip into defense mode and will not be forthcoming with vital information that could be the root cause of the issue. If, on the other hand, the issue is related to personal hygiene or other more sensitive issues such as bad habits, talking too loud on the phone, or any number of issues, then a certain level of decorum is called for and will be appreciated by the employee. Still, at the same time, be specific about the issue at hand.

I once observed a manager place a bottle of mouthwash on an employee's desk while the employee was in the restroom. Upon her return, she discovered the mouthwash and became noticeably embarrassed and confused as to who would do such a thing. Because of the manager's poor choice of communication in this situation, the employee withdrew from face-to-face communication and started using the telephone. This severely impacted her work performance, as she went out of her way to avoid contact with other employees and customers.

Had the manager had the courage simply to call her into his office and privately discuss the issue, he would have discovered that her problem was due to a medical condition, and she had been undergoing medical treatment to solve the problem. The issue would have been between the manager and her, and she would not have been embarrassed in front of her colleagues.

Personal problems aside, occasionally, you may have to deal with issues such as excessive breaks, missed deadlines, and poor work habits among many other possible issues. In cases such as these, take the time to compile a list of specific behavior issues and seriously consider what the acceptable resolution will be.

Often managers will jump right in and start discussing a behavioral issue with an employee with no real plan or desired result. They will talk to the employee in hopes that the problem will go away simply because they discussed the issue.

You need to have a well thought out resolution to the issue so that when the employee walks out of your office, he has a defined plan and goal. He has a measurable set of conditions that he knows he must meet, along with a defined deadline. It is important to allow adequate time for the employee to adjust specific behaviors.

Regardless of the type of behavioral issue with which you are dealing, it is important that the employee walk out of your office with a list of specific behaviors or performance issues that you find unacceptable, along with achievable goals that need to be reached to get back into your good graces.

Give Them a Warning

Unfortunately, you may encounter an employee that, for one reason or another, discussion and planning fall short of resolving the issue at hand. When this happens, it may be time to escalate the issue to the next level.

An employee warning has several uses. If you previously discussed the issue at hand with the employee and created a plan complete with timetable for correcting the issue as I explained earlier, then a written warning would be the next step. First, it informs the employee that there is still an issue with his behavior or performance. Second, it gives the company formal documentation to track an employee's problem and hopefully their progress in resolving the issue. Third, it tells the employee that serious change needs to be taken.

As previously discussed, it is best to perform this type of employee discipline in private. Assuming you had created an action plan during the discussion phase, now is the time to review that plan with the employee to determine what went wrong. Often, the employee does not take the issue seriously and does not try very hard to meet the predetermined progress milestones, or his manager was not vigilant in overseeing the employee's progress. In either case, you are now faced with a more difficult situation.

If, at this point, you have decided that further discussion is not the answer, then it is time for a formal warning. Warnings can be either verbal or written. In either case, you and the employee will need to address why the original plan failed to produce results by documenting where the shortfalls were, and what will be done to correct the issues.

By the time you have gotten to this phase in the process, I recommend using written warnings, as they become documentation of the employee progress and/or failure of progress and can be invaluable should the issue go beyond the warning phase. If, however, you choose to pursue a verbal warning, then that is fine as well.

Remember, however, that as time marches on, memories tend to fade, and the verbal warning you give today may be long forgotten later on should the issue arise once again. If it does, you may find yourself in a *he said, she said* situation. Therefore, if you do choose a verbal warning, do not plan to bring it up anytime in the future, because when you do, it will be easy for the employee to use poor memory as a crutch. You can download a warning form from my Web site at www.jaylabonte.com if you need one.

As you discuss the warning with the employee, make it perfectly clear that if the performance or behavior in question does not improve, they may be terminated. Bear in mind that it is important that termination be a viable option. All too often, I have seen managers use termination as a threat with an employee that they do not intend to terminate for any number of reasons. If termination is not a real possibility, then find some other consequence for continued poor performance or behavior—perhaps a one-day suspension or loss of a bonus. Check with your company's human resources department for other ideas that will not get you in trouble with employment laws. The point is that the potential consequences must be real; otherwise, they are merely idle threats, and their behavior will not change.

A Day Off ...

When a written warning does not work, managers are often placed in the difficult position of deciding whether termination is an option. In many cases today, it is not an option, or the offense simply does not warrant termination at this point. So what is a manager to do?

Often, I have seen companies endure poor employee behavior simply because they could not terminate an employee or felt the employee was too valuable to terminate. First, if you have an employee that is too valuable to terminate, then you have a much more serious problem on your hands. You should consider cross training your employees so that you do not have all your eggs in one basket, so to speak. However, if you find yourself in a situation where termination is not something you feel should be considered at this time, you could consider other disciplinary tactics such as giving the problem employee the day off.

I can hear you now. A day off—how is giving an employee a day off considered discipline? Let me explain; you are not giving him a day off to do whatever he wants. You are giving him a day out of the office with a task. The task is to think long and hard about his performance or behavior, and he needs to make a decision—a decision he must provide you with the following day. That decision is to make a choice—he can choose to correct whatever problem has brought him to this point in the disciplinary process, or he can choose to seek other employment.

Often, I am asked whether this suspension should be a paid day or an unpaid day. I suggest a paid day for two reasons. First, it just is not practical not to pay a salaried employee for a day. Second, the loss of pay can compound the employee's problem, creating a bitter individual, as the loss of pay is affecting his family. Your aim is to correct the employee's performance, not punish his family.

If there is no loss of pay because of the suspension, the employee is obligated to continue working for the company and has a responsibility to the company. In this case, he may not be doing his regular job, but he is working on a company task—the task of making a choice to improve his performance or behavior or find new employment. It is a decision day.

The Ultimate Form of Discipline

Employee termination is the ultimate form of disciplinary action.

Having to look someone in the eye and tell him he no longer has a source of income is one of the toughest things you will ever have to do. It is often as hard on the person doing the firing as it is on the person being fired.

I still remember the first time I had to fire one of my team members. It was on a Monday. He was an excellent programmer and a trustworthy individual, but I had to plan for the worse. You never know how someone will take this type of news. On Sunday, we disabled his logins and boxed up his personal belongings. It was the one of the most difficult acts I have ever done, and I felt terrible.

Every precaution was taken, and the utmost care had been taken during the previous months. Documentation was thorough and personnel files complete. Nothing should have been a surprise to him, and I was sure he suspected it.

No matter what I told myself, it did not make it any easier. I could not sleep a wink that night. I kept playing the scenarios over in my mind. What should I say? How should I say it? Should I be stern? What happens if he gets angry? What happens if he gets violent? My mind ran wild with *what ifs*.

That morning, I delivered the message as best I could and was relieved to see that he took it well, or at least pretended to take it well.

It never gets any easier either, no matter how many times you have to let someone go. It is just as difficult each time.

It is an unfortunate situation when it comes time to terminate a team member, even one that has been *poisoning the well* and bringing down the team. However, when all else fails, it comes down to what is best for the team.

Over the years, I have had the unfortunate responsibility to terminate employees many times, and I have witnessed many managers terminate employees. Terminating an employee is a delicate process in which the most important factor is leaving each person with his dignity intact. You do not need to humiliate him, but at the same time, you cannot leave any room for debate.

Depending on the circumstances, you may want to offer him a choice. If the termination is such that it is highly unlikely the employee will receive unemployment compensation, then you may want to offer him the chance to resign, thereby allowing him to exit with his dignity intact.

On the other hand, if he refuses to resign, or there is the possibility that he may be entitled to employment compensation, such as in a layoff situation, then firing is the better option.

Plan the event with the same detail that you would a meeting with a multi-million dollar client; leave nothing to chance. Select a private meeting room close to an exit but away from the workforce. Remove any potential weapons, such as statues or paperweights. Yes, that is what I said—potential weapons. Even with the best planning, there is still no way of knowing how an employee will take the news that his source of income has been taken away from him. Lastly, do not get between the employee and the doorway. It is best to keep a large object such as a conference table or desk separating you from the employee.

Take the time to prepare everything in advance, including the written termination notice and severance check, and arrange for the employee's locker or desk to be cleaned out for him. You do not want to give the employee any reason to return. It saves everyone embarrassment and eliminates any potential scenes.

Every employee is different and it is difficult to know how someone will take the news of being terminated. Do your best to identify how the employee may take this type of news. If you feel the employee is likely to break down in tears, then arrange to have emotional support at hand. If, however, history shows the employee has a tendency for violence, have a security officer or an off-duty police officer standing by.

I have often witnessed normally calm people turn violent upon hearing they have been terminated. Another concern is often the next business day. On at least three occasions, I have observed the employee or the employee's spouse enter the business the next day threatening violence. If you feel this is a possibility, especially after a large layoff, you may want to consider hiring an off-duty police officer to stand by for a few days after the layoff. It can be a small price to pay in light of today's economic troubles.

Get the Job Done

There is only one thing worse than firing an employee who is likely to get emotional, angry, or violent, and that is not firing him. Holding onto a team member who is not performing or who has behavior issues can and will bring down the entire team and send the signal to the other team members that they can get away with similar behavior.

Assuming you have made the decision to terminate your problem employee, then the best advice I can give you is simply to get the job done. Do not rationalize hanging on until the end of the day or until conditions are right because the truth is, no time will ever be the right time.

When the time comes to sit down with the employee, do not get caught up in the employee's emotions. Have a witness present during the meeting in case the employee threatens retaliation. It is best to have someone from human resources sit in. Once you are ready, proceed with the following:

- Tell the employee that you are terminating him, and you expect him to leave the office at a certain time. It is best to have him leave as quickly as possible with perhaps enough time for him to make the rounds to say good-bye. However, exercise caution as I have seen disgruntled employees use this time to cause as much covert damage as possible.

- Explain that firing is *for cause*, but avoid going into detail about the grounds for the termination. You do not want to start an argument. Just point out that the employee did not attain the goals you wanted him to reach in his last performance review. If the employee objects or becomes defensive, simply say "I'm sorry, but my mind is made up." If you have followed my guidelines for counseling and warning, he will expect this action and will not argue it.

- Explain how much severance pay, if any, you will provide and what other benefits he will be entitled to after he leaves your employment. In most cases, the human resources department handles this best.

- Explain to him what you will say should anyone call and ask for a job reference. Be sure you have spoken with the human resources department and or an employment law attorney first and have agreed on the exact wording. This may actually give the employee some level of comfort knowing what you will tell prospective employers should they call to confirm past employment.

Reassign the Employee Duties Promptly

Terminating a team member is not only difficult for you and the terminated employee but for the team. They will feel a sense of loss and a feeling of uncertainty about what the future will bring and how this termination will affect them.

As soon as the terminated employee has left, you should call a team meeting and tell them that the employee is no longer working for the company, without getting into details about the reason. In fact, you should send an e-mail out companywide as well so that everyone knows the employee is no longer with the company.

In some cases, and depending on what the employee's interaction with clients and vendors was, you may want to notify some clients and vendors that the employee has moved on and is no longer associated with the company and provide them with a new contact person on your team. This will prevent the rumor mill from starting stories and will prepare employees and other associates for any negative phone calls and or e-mails they may receive from the terminated employee.

During this team meeting, you should discuss the impact and how this termination affects the team, which is a great segue into reassigning the terminated employee's duties to other team members.

Reassigning duties quickly is the key to calming other team members' fears as to how the termination affects their positions. Try to distribute duties evenly among team members so that no one feels the change is unfairly affecting him. If you do not have a new duty for some team members, tell them so; otherwise, they may feel that they may be next on the chopping block and that is why they did not get a task assigned to them.

Career Advancement

Most everyone wants to advance in his or her career for more money, more responsibility, more challenges, more education, or more power. Some want more of one thing than the other, but most everyone wants to advance. Even those that claim they are satisfied with their present career position would not mind more pay or more knowledge. George Carlin once said, "Most people work hard enough not to get fired and get paid just enough not to quit."

The key here is to motivate your team to work harder because they want to work harder, not because it is required.

Early in my career as a programmer, I worked hard. I burned the midnight oil, and I did not sleep until I solved some problem or developed an impressive new user interface. All of this hard work, of course, was rewarded with raises and other great benefits.

At the time, I thought the respect and raises I received from my boss and other employees were due to my abilities as a programmer and my unique way of solving problems. Those certainly did contribute to it, but as my supervisor told me, "You make managing very easy. You tackle the problems that arise and solve them with total confidence." He then told me his secret to management. He said, "Management is easy. Simply surround yourself with the best team and cover their butts, and they will cover yours."

It was at that moment I realized that, although I had the talent, it was my attitude and my respect that mattered the most. I had a can-do attitude and a passion to solve problems, and this is what they wanted from me.

Many years later, when I was the Information Systems Manager, I was looking for a junior programmer to fill a newly created position. I placed an ad in the local paper for the position and received about thirty résumés. I narrowed the list down to three candidates. All three were in their early twenties.

The first one, whom I will call "Carl," had an impressive résumé. On paper, he appeared to know his way around a computer. As he stepped into my office, I noticed that Carl was dressed about average—a polo shirt, Docker-style slacks, and a clean-shaven face. He presented himself well. Unfortunately, he opened his mouth and started to babble on and on about how wonderful he was and how impressed his former employers were with his abilities, which raised several questions on my part as to why he was not still employed with them. It turned out he was exactly where I might have been had I not realized early on that technical skills can be learned by nearly anyone, but passion is something you either have for your work or you do not, and he did not.

The second candidate I will call "Ron." Ron was an interesting, yet odd fellow. Ron entered my office wearing a white, long-sleeved shirt with a very nice pullover sweater, nice dress pants, a belt that was twisted halfway around, one white sock and one red sock, and athletic shoes, and yes, they both matched. Ron had sort of wild hair that was indescribable and a goatee-style beard.

His résumé was impressive to say the least. He was intelligent, well spoken, communicated well, and about halfway through the interview, I was thinking, “This is the guy.” He answered my questions intelligently; he did not babble on, or look off in space and ignore me. He made eye contact the whole time I was telling him about the job. He never once flinched when I told him about some of the long hours or the hectic deadlines. He was... asleep! Yes, it turns out he was a narcoleptic. He did not hear a word I said. Unfortunately, his condition would have been dangerous for employment as the company was a metals fabricator, and we could not have someone falling asleep with heavy equipment moving about while he programmed various systems.

The third and final candidate for the day was a young man I will refer to as “Leon.” Leon did not have an impressive résumé at all. In fact, the only programming experience he had was on his own computer at home. His résumé indicated his last job was repairing washing machines and other household appliances.

The truth is I asked him to come for an interview because I was curious. Why would a washer repairman with no experience apply for a junior programming position? I figured this would be a rather interesting interview, and perhaps I could offer him some advice—perhaps to enroll in a programming class.

Leon walked into my office, clean-shaven, wearing a nice suit, his shoes were polished, and he was obviously nervous. I asked him to take a seat and tell me why he wanted this job since his résumé obviously was not that of a programmer. He spoke very eloquently and informed me that if he only looked for jobs he knew how to do, he would never learn anything else. He informed me he loved to write programs on his home computer and felt that if he could have this job, he would be honored to have the opportunity to learn from us and do what he loves. I hired him on the spot!

It was obvious Leon had the passion I had when I was younger, and I instinctively knew his passion would make up for what he lacked in experience.

Leon left after three years and was one of the most enthusiastic and teachable individuals I have ever had the pleasure to know. About five years later, I ran into him at a convention in Las Vegas. He thanked me for the opportunity and told he was now an IT manager for a company in Tampa, Florida.

Leon is the perfect example of attitude over experience. Nobody knows what the future holds, and experience is simply a list of things people have done. The important thing is how they got the experience and how they performed under pressure.

To advance one's career, one must take on new challenges. By new challenges, I do not mean tasks that use the same skills you have been using, but challenges that develop new skills.

I once had a supervisor that tasked me with just this sort of challenge. I was a senior level programmer specializing in inventory control systems when he walked into my office and asked me how I liked writing inventory control software. I told him it was great and I enjoyed it, thinking this might be a trick question. Truth be told, I was bored. I had been writing inventory software for years, and I was getting burnt out.

He then surprised me with a new project. He said, "I see you've become bored and think you need a new challenge. I want you to develop a telemarketing system for a cemetery." He handed me a book on telemarketing and said, "All you have to do is figure out how the hell a cemetery does telemarketing!" He then added a final comment, telling me that if I figured out how to do that, it would look good on my résumé. I figured it out, and enjoyed every minute of that project.

Setting Goals for Advancement

Many employees do not fully understand how to advance their careers. They assume that performing their current job well in conjunction with someone higher up the corporate ladder leaving will result in their ascending the ladder of success. They also wrongly assume that since business often focuses on management, they want to be in management. Often, they are unprepared for that jump or simply cannot figure out how to take that next step.

Often, they are not aware of any incremental steps between their current position and that management position they seek. Often, just informing your team of the various possibilities of advancement can go a long way in helping your team advance. Laying out the various steps they can take can bring many possibilities into focus.

If you want to build that excellent team that has that *we can handle anything you throw at us* attitude, then you need to groom your team members for advancement. In many organizations, when a project is completed and rolled out, often someone may receive a promotion in conjunction with the project. In fact, one of the project requirements may involve having someone accompany the rollout of the project to manage it on a continual basis. An example might be a software project that is completed and rolled out to the public. The project manager or the entire team may take on new responsibility dealing with maintenance and customer support.

As the team leader, you need to help your team advance. You need to help them identify the skills they will need to handle advancement and help them set goals for that advancement. Some team members may need help with various aspects such as personal productivity, forging client relationships, dealing with office politics, or motivating others. Your task as team leader is to guide them and help them establish the skills they need.

Often, I hear project managers claim that if they provide too much training, they fear that team members will jump ship and find other employment. This is a possibility. However, if you treat your team well and provide a constant path for growth and advancement, it is highly unlikely they will leave. After all, why leave a good job with great training and advancement possibilities for another job that may not offer such advancement possibilities.

I have researched many surveys, and more money is rarely the reason people seek other employment. The primary reasons cited by those seeking alternative employment are better advancement potential, ability to learn and expand, and more respect. Even if your team members do eventually seek alternative employment, by establishing an advancement path, you will at least be able to plan for who leaves and when.

Who knows, maybe they will actually stay longer out of respect and fear of landing at a company that does not offer such advancement possibilities. This type of planning can actually make your team see your company as a sought after place of employment.

Goals

Goals are an important part of leading any team. However, when I speak of individual goals, I am not talking about individual project goals or task-related goals. I am talking about personal goals—the goals your team members have for themselves.

Many people ask me at this point, "Why should I care about employees' personal goals?" They go on and claim that the company's goals are all that matter. I have even heard managers state, "I don't care about other people's personal goals; from 8:00 am to 5:00 pm, my goals are all that count!" or "I don't have time to worry about someone else's goals; right now, our project goals are being missed, and that's all that counts!"

What is interesting about most of these managers with missed goals and delayed projects is that none of them have any interest in their team members' goals. As a result, their teams do not produce, or they produce too slowly.

The obvious question here is why. Why should I care? Why do my team members' goals matter? And why are my project goals being missed? The answer is rather clear, at least to me. Can you see the common thread of all these why, why, why questions? They are all about "me" or "I" and none of them is about the team members. Other people's goals do not motivate people; their own goals motivate them.

The reason most projects never reach their goal is that the project's goal is not in alignment with the team members' personal goals. In other words, if you want your team's goals to be realized, then you must tie the team's goals to the members' personal goals.

Let me paraphrase a statement made by Rensis Likert, an American educator and organizational psychologist best known for his research on management styles. The greater the goals of a group tie into the goals of the individual, the greater is the motivation among the members to achieve the goals of the group, and the greater the probability that the group will achieve its goals.

Take the time to explore the personal goals of your team members and help define their goals. By doing this, you can help them realize their personal goals by tying them into the project goals which in turn will result in the teams goals being realized as well. In the end, you will have a more motivated employee that feels productive and, at the same time, may feel he is taking advantage of the company because he is advancing his own goals. These can be a huge boost to morale as well.

For example, let's say you have a project that requires sending someone for training. Take the time to find the team member that has a personal interest in acquiring the knowledge. Sometimes, the natural choice for training is not always the best choice.

I have seen many managers take a training course because they thought it was their job to learn it, or they simply felt it would provide job security. As a result, they became bogged down with too much to do and too little time in which to do it—not to mention the fact that they also became un-promotable as well.

There is a point when a manager can taint his own chances for a promotion by becoming too valuable to an organization. Do not make that mistake. Take the time to align the company goals with your team members' goals. In the end, you will have a happier, more productive team that will make you shine.

Room to Grow

Many employers have the idea that employees should maintain a narrow focus and concentrate strictly on their specific jobs. Employers fear that expanding employees' knowledge and skills, especially an employee in an essential position, would result in the employee seeking other employment. The reality is that most employees are already looking for other employment. They are seeking new experiences, expanded knowledge, and career advancement.

Withholding educational opportunities, opportunities to enhance skills, and access to knowledge are surefire ways to ensure that an employee, in fact, will leave in pursuit of an employer where he can obtain career advancement. If, however, you collaborate with your team members and formulate an advancement strategy, either within the organization or with someone else, the result will be a more appreciative and loyal team member.

Promotions

Promoting the wrong employee is easy and happens all the time. Promoting the right employee is, however, much more difficult and can mean the difference between a successful team and a total disaster.

I am always amazed at how many companies approach promotions. The list of wrong reasons for promoting someone can be rather lengthy. Here are six poor reasons for promoting someone:

1. "He's a friend of mine."
2. "He's worked here a long time..."
3. "She seems bored; maybe a promotion will get her motivated."
4. "If we don't promote him, he may leave."
5. "We really need someone in that position."
6. "The only way to give her a raise is to promote her."

None of these excuses for promotion needs further explanation, but the list goes on. Another temptation is to be the white knight to an employee with problems. In this scenario, a team member may be dealing with some personal issues, so the thinking goes that promoting him will help him solve his problems in some way. There is nothing worse than promoting someone in hopes of getting rid of a problem.

It is important to realize that competence does not mean someone should receive a promotion or is capable of handling that promotion. Many employers equate solid job skills as a factor in promotion. Do not get me wrong; it is great to promote someone with solid job skills, but skills alone do not insure success in a higher position with greater responsibility.

Technical skills should be of secondary importance when promoting someone to a new position. The primary focus should be the specific skills required for the new position, such as communications, team leadership, mentoring, ability to motivate, and any other skills required for success in the new position. Therefore, it is important to take the time to determine what you think are important skills in employees with promotion potential.

Take the time to determine why you would like to promote an employee rather than hire a new employee to fill the position. All too often, companies do not give any detailed thought about the attributes they look for in employees worthy of promotion.

Once you have determined that you will be promoting rather than hiring a new employee, take the time to let all your employees know what you are looking for in a candidate. Once you have notified the employees that you will be promoting someone, encourage them to make suggestions as to whom they feel would be a good fit. Often, fellow employees know more about a potential candidate's personality than his supervisor does.

Employees should never be surprised about a promotion. If they are surprised, then they may resent the person you promoted, or even worse, you may have overlooked the perfect candidate.

Another area of concern is the buddy factor. Not everyone can make the transition from buddy to boss. This also includes the employee that may have to report to his *buddy* now. It is important to understand how the promotion will be viewed by the other employees that may have to report to the person you promote.

While considering the potential candidates' strengths, be sure to evaluate his weaknesses also. One major problem companies cite is ignoring various weaknesses, thinking they will simply work themselves out, and not evaluating how an employee will handle various problems.

Now that you have diligently evaluated all the potential candidates, you have determined all the social consequences to the promotion, and you are ready to promote someone, do not be surprised if he refuses the promotion.

Employees can turn down a promotion for many reasons, ranging from travel requirements, family reasons, to lack of confidence that they can do the job, or they simply do not think they are the best choice. Whatever the reason, respect their decision.

Using Your New Skills

I have led many teams in my life and have found that nearly every team member excels at something. Often these individuals are assigned tasks that either do not interest them or do not make use of their hidden genius.

As the team's leader, it is your responsibility to identify each team member's hidden genius, nurture it, and put it to use. This may require the redistribution of tasks and other responsibilities, but the benefit to you and your team will be immeasurable.

Sometimes, you may find that a team member's hidden genius does not always suit a business-related task or responsibility. If this is the case, then keep looking, most likely your team members have hidden genius of which they are not aware. Find it and cultivate it.

Any endeavor you take that involves other people is a team effort, and the success or failure of that endeavor depends on your ability to lead that team. As you work to advance your organization, you will need to depend on your team. The larger the organization, the more teams you will have, each with specific responsibilities, and the harder your job will be to keep those team members motivated and producing. It is therefore in your best interest to do whatever is necessary to keep your team members productive.

If you follow the methods I have presented, you will discover a team with a can-do attitude, a team that is ready to follow you and trust in your leadership. I wish you great success in leading your team and your quest for excellence. Cultivate Your Guiding Genius and become the leader you want to be, and more importantly, the leader your team will follow, trust, and respect. Doing so will yield a team that can accomplish whatever goals you set. As you venture out and place these methods into practice, remember this, a team is most effective when its members can compliment each other without embarrassment and disagree without fear.

References

Abagnale, Frank W. 1980. *Catch me if you can: The true story of a real fake.* New York: Grosset & Dunlap.

Alfaro,Mercedes. 2008. First Impression Management.

http://www.firstimpressionmanagement.com (Accesses April 15, 2008)

Blanchard, Kenneth, and Spencer Johnson. 1981. *The one minute manager.* New York: Berkley Publishing Group.

Bowditch, James L., and Buono, Anthony F. 1997. *A primer on organizational behavior.* 4th ed. New York: John Wiley & Sons.

Buchanan, Leigh. 2001.Managing one-to-one. *Inc. Magazine,* October.

Coser, L. A. 1956. *The functions of social conflict: An examination of the concept of social conflict and its use in empirical sociological research.* New York: The Free Press.

Covey, Stephen R. 1989. *The 7 habits of highly effective people.* New York: Free Press.

Detz, Joan. 2000. *It's not what you say, it's how you say it: Ready-to-use advice for presentations, speeches, and other speaking occasions, large and small.* New York: St. Martin's Griffin.

Deutsh, M. 1969. Conflicts: Productive and destructive. *Journal of Social Issues,* 25 (1), 7–41.

Fisher, K., Rayner, S., and Belgard, W. 1995. *Tips for teams: A ready reference for solving common team problems.* New York: McGraw-Hill, Inc.

Fox, Jeffrey J. 2002. *How to become a great boss: The rules for getting and keeping the best employees.* New York: Hyperion Books.

Harkavy, Daniel S. 2007. *Becoming a coaching leader: The proven strategy for building your own team of champions.* Nashville, TN: Thomas Nelson.

Harrell, Keith 2007. CONNECT: *Building success through people, purpose, and performance.* New York: HarperCollins.

Johnston, Dr. Joni. 2000. Lessons from the humor police: How to evaluate workplace humor. Work Relationships. http://www.workrelationships.com/site/articles/humoratwork.htm (accessed July 10, 2006).

Kaihla, Paul. 2006. Best-kept secrets of the world's best companies. *Business 2.0,* March 23.

Kaplan, Simone. 2002. What to do when morale is low. *CIO Magazine,* May 1.

Kemp, Sid. 2004. *Perfect solutions for difficult employee situations.* Columbia, OH: McGraw-Hill.

Kezsbom, D. S. 1992. Re-opening Pandora's box: Sources of project conflict in the '90s. *Industrial Engineering.*

Kohn, Alfie. 1993. For best results, forget the bonus. *New York Times,* October.

Kroc, Ray 1992. *Grinding it out: The making of McDonald's.* Chicago: Contemporary Books.

Levine, Terri. 2006. *The successful coach: Insider secrets to becoming a top coach.* Hoboken, NJ: Wiley.

Lewis, Bob. 2003. Survival guide—Calculating the value of IT. *InfoWorld.com,* February 12.

Lundine, Susan. 2000. *The Orlando Business Journal.* Cited in Jim Sullivan, Nation's Restaurant News. August 21, 2000. http://www.gametime.net.au/online2.pdf

Maxwell, John C. 2007. *The 21 irrefutable laws of leadership.* Nashville, TN: Thomas Nelson.

McGarvey, Robert. 1996. Fire 'em up—Motivating unproductive employees. *Entrepreneur Magazine,* March.

Nelson, Bob. 1999. Incentives for all generations. *Inc. Magazine,* February.

Nelson, M. 1995. Interpersonal team leadership skills. *Hospital Material Management Quarterly.*

Pacelli, Lonnie. 2006. Thirteen tips to effective upward management. *FT Press: Financial Times*, November 16. http://www.ftpress.com/articles/article.aspx?p=668004

Shepard, Glen. 2005. *How to manage difficult employees.* Hoboken, NJ: Wiley.

Solomon, Richard, Neil Davidson, and Elaine Solomon. 1993. *The handbook for the fourth R: Relationship activities for cooperative and collegial learning.* Columbia, MD: National Institute for Relationship Training.

Stack, Jack. 1997. Measuring morale. *Inc. Magazine*, January.

Star Trek II. Directed by Robert Wise. Hollywood, CA: Paramount Pictures.

Strauss, William, and Neil Howe. 1991. *Generations: The history of America's future, 1584 to 2069.* New York: William Morrow and Company, Inc.

Stulberg, J. B. 1987. *Taking charge/managing conflict.* Lexington, MA: Lexington Books.

Thamhain, H., and D. L. Wilemon. 1975. Conflict management in project life cycles. *Sloan Management Review.*

Varney, G. H. 1989. *Building productive teams: An action guide and resource book.* San Francisco, CA: Jossey-Bass, Inc.

Villano, Matt. 2001. How to fire people. *CIO Magazine*, April 15.

Vitale, Joe. 2007. *Buying trances*. Hoboken, NJ: John Wiley & Sons, Inc.

———. 2008. *Inspired marketing*. Hoboken, NJ: John Wiley & Sons, Inc.

Weiss, D. H. 1997. Four steps for managing team storms. *Getting Results for the Hands-on Manager*, 42 (7), 7.

Williams, Paula Gamonal. 2007. "How (and why!) to make yourself obsolete." Ravenwerks, March 3. http://www.ravenwerks.com/leadership/succession.htm

Wilson, Tracy V. 2007. How geniuses work: An introduction to how geniuses work. *Howstuffworks*. http://people.howstuffworks.com.

Wuorio, Jeff. 2001. Promoting employees: How to get it right. Microsoft Small Business Center, February 1. http://www.microsoft.com/smallbusiness/resources/management/employee-relations/promoting-employees-how-to-get-it-right.aspx

Yates, Phil. 2002. Regional business managers—Are you *managing* or *leading* your team. Pharmaceutical and Medical Sales Jobs for UK Medical, Pharmaceutical, Healthcare and Scientific. http://www.allaboutmedicalsales.com/articles/managing_leading_cts_040102.html (accessed March 23, 2006).

Index

E

T

U

V

W

About the Author

Jay LaBonte is no stranger to team leadership, having more than 29 years of experience managing teams of all sizes in various industries. As a product of the booming computer industry in the late 1970s, Mr. LaBonte began his career as a systems programmer/analyst in the aerospace manufacturing industry in Pompano Beach, Florida.

Over the next three decades, Mr. LaBonte was constantly recognized for his ability to manage diverse teams in various business disciplines such as real estate, restaurant management, cemetery management, oil and gas ventures, and marina management. Mr. LaBonte eventually became the Director of Information Technology for a large multinational aerospace metals distributor with many government contracts, including NASA's space shuttle program.

Mr. LaBonte then founded AccuTrac Corporation, a software development firm, where he and his team designed and sold state-of-the-art inventory control systems, specializing in the aerospace industry. Because of this work,

Mr. LaBonte has been featured as the cover story in various business journals regarding the future of inventory control systems.

After leaving AccuTrac Corporation, Mr. LaBonte gained a broad range of experience in the PEO (Professional Employment Organization) industry where he spent over a decade designing, developing, and managing software development teams tasked with creating some of the most advanced employee deployment systems. These systems processed job placements and payroll for tens of thousands of employees on a weekly basis.

Throughout his career, Mr. LaBonte has been invited to write many articles for various magazines and business journals about the Internet and child Internet safety, inventory control systems, and check fraud prevention. As an author, he has shown countless parents and schools how to protect children while surfing the Internet through his book *Parents Guide to the Internet*, and he has helped scores of individuals and businesses protect themselves from check fraud with his book *The Truth about Check Fraud*.

Mr. LaBonte holds a bachelor's degree in Information Management Systems and a master's degree in Computer Information Systems from Columbia Southern University. In addition, his work in the PEO industry led Mr. LaBonte to earn his certification as an Employment Law Specialist.

www.ingramcontent.com/pod-product-compliance
Lightning Source LLC
LaVergne TN
LVHW091053080826
845145LV00002B/725

* 9 7 8 0 6 1 5 2 6 4 2 5 7 *